The Family Guide
to Children's Television

OTHER ACT PUBLICATIONS

Action for Children's Television, edited by Evelyn Kaye Sarson

Bibliography and Summary of Research in Children's Television

Concerned Parents Speak Out on Children's Television by F. Earle Barcus

Mothers' Attitudes Toward Children's Television Programs and Commercials by Daniel Yankelovitch

Network Children's Programming: A Content Analysis of Black and Minority Treatment on Children's Television by Gilbert Mendelson and Morrissa Young

Network Programming and Advertising in the Saturday Children's Hours by F. Earle Barcus

Programming and Advertising Practices in Television Directed to Children by Ralph Jennings

Programming and Advertising Practices in Television Directed to Children—Another Look by Ralph and Carol Jennings

Romper Room: An Analysis by F. Earle Barcus

Saturday Children's Television by F. Earle Barcus

Second National Symposium on Children and Television

"*Who Is Talking to Our Children?*" edited by Evelyn Kaye Sarson and Peggy Charren (joint publication of ACT and ERIC Clearinghouse on Media and Technology, Stanford, Ca.)

The Family Guide to Children's Television

WHAT TO WATCH, WHAT TO MISS, WHAT TO CHANGE AND HOW TO DO IT

Evelyn Kaye

*Under the guidance of Action for Children's Television
with the cooperation of the American Academy of Pediatrics*

With Illustrations by Edward Frascino

PANTHEON BOOKS

A Division of Random House / New York

Copyright © 1974 by Action for Children's
Television, Inc.

Illustrations copyright © 1974
by Random House, Inc.

All rights reserved under International and Pan-
American Copyright Conventions. Published in the
United States by Pantheon Books, a division of
Random House, Inc., New York, and simultaneously
in Canada by Random House of Canada Limited.

All royalties from the sale of this book will go to
Action for Children's Television.

Library of Congress Cataloging in Publication Data

Kaye, Evelyn, 1937–
The Family Guide to Children's Television: What to
Watch, What to Miss, What to Change and How
to Do It.

"Under the guidance of Action for Children's
Television with the cooperation of the American
Academy of Pediatrics."

Bibliography: pp. 156–66.
1. Television and children. 2. Television programs
—United States. I. Action for Children's Television.
II. American Academy of Pediatrics. III. Title.
HQ784.T4K38   791.45'5   73–18726
ISBN 0–394–49157–2
ISBN 0–394–70637–4 (pbk.)

Manufactured in the United States of America

First Edition

WITH SPECIAL THANKS

—*to Peggy Charren and Carol Liebman*

—*to those professionals working with children who care about television*

—*to those TV broadcasters who care about children*

—*to producers, writers, advertisers, journalists, and parents who have shared their advice and experiences*

—*to all the supporters and members of ACT who have shown their limitless encouragement for ACT's ideals*

—*and to my husband, Christopher Sarson, and two TV-watching children, Katrina and David, who started it all.*

ACKNOWLEDGMENTS

Grateful acknowledgment is made to the following for permission to reprint previously published material:

Broadcasting Publications Inc.: for "A Short Course in Cable, 1974," from the April 22, 1974, issue of Broadcasting *Magazine. Copyright © 1974 by Broadcasting Publications Inc.*

Leo Burnett Company, Inc., and National Dairy Council: for the reproduction of the "AWARD" public service TV spot storyboard.

Letty C. Pogrebin: for excerpts from her speech included in "Who is Talking to Our Children?" *Copyright © 1972 by Letty Cottin Pogrebin.*

Marsha O'Bannon Prowitt: for material from Guide to Citizen Action in Radio and Television *by Marsha O'Bannon Prowitt. Copyright © 1971 by Marsha O'Bannon Prowitt.*

Redbook: *for "How to Tame the TV Monster" by T. Berry Brazelton, from the April 1972, issue of* Redbook. *Copyright © 1972, The McCall Publishing Company.*

Dr. Lee Salk: for excerpt reprinted from December, 1972, issue of McCalls *Magazine, "You and Your Family" by Dr. Lee Salk.*

Topps Chewing Gum, Inc.: for use of the pictures from six bubble gum cards.

Contents

Preface

HOW TO TAME
THE TV MONSTER

A PEDIATRICIAN'S ADVICE*

T. BERRY BRAZELTON, M.D.

For a long time we have known that television plays an important role in the lives of our children. But only within the last few years have we begun to understand how powerful its influence really is, and many of us are worried. Recognizing the problem is one thing; solving it is another.

As a parent and as a pediatrician, I think the situation is not hopeless—difficult, yes, but not hopeless. I think there are some positive steps we can take to control this monster medium. Before we get into practical things you can do, however, let me first sketch the basis of my concern about television—about what it is and what it does.

My uneasiness is related to my studies of newborn babies. When a baby is born he is thrust from a protective existence inside his mother's womb into a hostile world outside. And given the

* Reprinted from *Redbook* magazine, where Dr. Brazelton is Contributing Editor.

fact that his major job involves simply trying to achieve some kind of equilibrium between himself and his new world, it has always amazed me that he is able to interact with his environment in the sophisticated way he does.

From the moment of birth an infant is able to take in and process information. He has a set of powerful mechanisms that allow him to control his universe, that allow him to respond with true discrimination to the sights and sounds around him. Since he might otherwise be at the mercy of all the stimuli to which he is exposed, he has the capacity to shut out those he judges "inappropriate."

A good example of what I mean by this comes from studies my coworkers and I carried out on newborn infants. We exposed a group of quietly resting babies to a disturbing visual stimulus—a bright operating room light—placed twenty-four inches from their heads. The light was on for three seconds, then off for one minute. The sequence was repeated twenty times. Throughout the test the babies were monitored for changes in their heartbeat, respiration, and brain waves. The first time the babies were exposed to the light stimulus, they were visibly startled; however, the intensity of their reaction decreased rapidly after a few times. By the tenth stimulus there were no changes in behavior, heartbeat, or respiration. By the fifteenth stimulus, sleep patterns appeared on the electroencephalogram, although it was clear that their eyes were still taking in the light. After twenty stimuli the babies awoke from their "induced" sleep to scream and thrash about.

Our experiment demonstrated that a newborn certainly is not at the mercy of his environment. He has a marvelous mechanism, a shutdown device, for dealing with disturbing stimuli: he can tune them out and go into a sleeplike state.

But if we can imagine the amount of energy a newborn baby expends in managing this kind of shutdown—energy he could put to better use—we can see how expensive this mechanism becomes when it is at work all the time.

And if we can realize this, I think, we may be getting to some understanding of the way television works and the way it affects small children. For just like the operating room light, television creates an environment that assaults and overwhelms the child; he can respond to it only by bringing into play his shutdown mechanism and thus becomes more passive.

I have observed this in my own children and I have seen it in other people's children. As they sat in front of a television set that was blasting away, watching a film of horrors of rapidly varying kinds, the children were completely quiet. Nails bitten, thumbs in mouth, faces pale, bodies tense—they were "hooked." If anyone interrupted, tapped a child on the shoulder to break through his state of rapt attention, he almost always would start and might even break down in angry crying. If he was led away from the set, he often dissolved into a combative, screaming, wildly thrashing mass.

Sigmund Freud's daughter Anna, an eminent child analyst, once called such behavior the "disintegration of the ego." Indeed, it seemed that whatever ego the child had was being sorely tested at a time like that. And I think the intensity of the reaction is clear evidence of the energy the child is putting into television watching and the shock he experiences when his attention, locked onto the screen, is broken into.

What bothers me most about television is the passivity it forces on children—the passivity that requires all activity to be produced for them, not by them. This, I feel, must have a powerful influence on any child's capacity to handle his normal aggressive impulses.

By the time a child is five or six years old, his fantasies are already as violent as those in any horror movie adults might construct, and his sexual fantasies can match anything presented in a grade C movie. The violence and adult forms of sexuality displayed on television mobilize these fantasies together with all the fear and anxiety that go with them.

I feel that this is one of the grave dangers of all the violence and sexual activity to which children are exposed—not that children are taught anything new by it, but that it strikes at very primitive impulses and mobilizes them, but leaves children with no way to give healthy expression to them. It comes down to the fact that television gives a child two choices: he can actively suppress his feelings or he can ineffectually play them out.

No wonder, then, that a child comes away from a television set believing that physical violence is a perfectly acceptable form of self-expression.

When we adults watch a television program—or a movie, for that matter—we do not always respond to what we see at the very moment it is being presented. Particularly if the material is disturbing or otherwise provocative, we often avoid immediate confrontation with it. But at a later time—an hour or so afterward, perhaps even the next day—we think about what we have seen. We reflect on it and compare it with our own experiences and our own store of ideas. We make sense of it first and then decide whether it is true for us.

But a child can't bring this sort of control to what he sees on television because his intellectual development hasn't taken him that far. He can't delay his response until he has mulled it over and tested it in his mind; he can't go back to it later. He is hooked into the experience of the moment; he gives himself totally to what he is viewing. The sights and sounds coming from the television screen wash over him then and there, and he can't protect himself, as we can, with intellectual detachment. He is forced to be a passive receiver.

In this sense, watching television for a child is totally different from reading—which might seem to be a similar passive activity. First of all, when a young child is reading he is putting into operation a skill he has newly acquired, and this in itself requires active participation on his part. As he struggles over each syllable, each word, he tries to relate it to other syllables and words, to other ideas he has learned. Though physically undemanding, reading requires a child to be mentally alert, to think, to bring to it something of himself.

And then, of course, the material presented in children's books is totally different from the kind that fills the television screen. Usually there is nothing so threatening, nothing so overwhelming, nothing so likely to stir up a child's unconscious fantasies. The authors and editors of children's literature are very scrupulous about this today. They are concerned about issues in child development: they are concerned about the age appropriateness of the material they publish, and often indicate that a book is recommended for children in a certain age bracket.

But this is not true for television, which for the most part does not take into account differences in age and in sensitivity among its young viewers. Adventure movies, even cartoons, may contain a level of violence and brutality that may not faze a seven- or eight-year-old, because at that age children can make a clearer distinction between what is real and true to life and what is not. But for a three- or four-year-old, such distinctions are not possible. Younger children may watch a cartoon show and come away disturbed and upset, though an adult—or an older child, for that matter—would consider it totally harmless. They cannot understand why Tom keeps hitting Jerry; they worry about how much it hurts. As a result, they themselves feel confused and vulnerable.

Still, even though we have to face the fact that television is not the best medium for a child to be exposed to, it does have an undeniable importance in the world today. From all the evidence it looks as if it is going to be around for a very long time, and we simply have to come to terms with it. But this does *not* mean that we as parents must throw up our hands in dismay and resignation. There are a few outstanding television programs for children, which means that "quality" is possible—if we demand it. Further, we *can* take some steps now to control what and how much television our children watch.

So now let's talk about what is right with television. The first time I was exposed to such programs as "Sesame Street," "Mister Rogers' Neighborhood," and, more recently, "The Electric Company," I began to be aware of the real potential for good that television programs can provide. Instead of being overwhelming, depleting, passive experiences, these programs demonstrated that small children could have warming times and learn exciting things—about their world and about themselves—in a period of television watching.

I first became aware of Mister Rogers when one of my four-year-old patients quoted him during his entire examination in my office. He was a boy who had been frightened of me on previous visits but was trying hard to master his anxiety this time. After I applied the cold stethoscope to his chest he nodded and said, "Just like Mister Rogers." When I used the earpiece, he winced but allowed it, saying, "Just like Mister Rogers." Before his shot he said, "Mister Rogers said it was okay for kids my age to cry for a shot. Do you think it is, Dr. Brazelton?"

Not to be outdone by this mythical Mister Rogers, I said, "Of course it is, Dan. And you know what? If you look the other way and let out a yell when I do it, it won't even hurt too much." These maneuvers worked to distract him. He yelled for a minute after the shot, then stopped and with a straight face said, "You're almost as good for kids as Mister Rogers."

By this time I wanted very much to congratulate a man who could prepare a child for a frightening experience by using a television program. By demonstrating what might happen on a visit to the doctor and by giving suggestions about how to face up to the anxiety and the pain it might bring, he had helped this boy through an ordeal and given him a chance to be proud of himself.

"Sesame Street" was literally shoved down my throat day after day by one three-year-old after another who read the letters from my eye chart with the musical phrase appropriate to each letter. I have watched "Sesame Street" myself, and I can see what a powerful teaching medium it is.

I do not feel that all the programs children watch must be "learning" experiences. Children really need to relax after a day in school; they must have some "throwaway" time. And I think they would find it in other ways—in comic books, for example— even if we could construct enough educational programs to fill the prime-time hours.

But it does seem that children really might prefer to be offered "good" and thoughtful programs for their selection. This is pointed up by the enormous number who watch repeats of "Sesame Street" or of "Mister Rogers' Neighborhood," who will cut off a war drama or a stirring love story their parents are watching to tune in to these repeats. My children say, "But, Dad, these programs are for *me*."

I feel that all you parents should try to acquaint yourselves with the programs that are being offered in your area, and then you can play an active part in your child's television viewing. Every Sunday or Monday, for example, you and your child could sit down with a guide to the week's shows and discuss them together. For each day select one or two programs that you both agree would be entertaining and worthwhile. If your child insists on something you don't think is suitable, gently but firmly discuss your reasons with him.

You could also make your selections on a daily basis, gearing your choices around the day's events and your child's mood. For a quiet day, he might need a soothing storyteller or a visit with Mister Rogers. For a learning day, "Sesame Street" or "The Electric Company" might be more appropriate. But whichever method you decide to use, after the program follow up with a discussion about what went on and an assessment of its quality. In this way you can make the experience a deeper and more meaningful one for your child.

Ideally, of course, it would be best if you could actually be there with your child and watch the program along with him, because your presence and obvious concern will give a deeper and more human dimension to what is essentially an isolating experience. Perhaps you could see to it that you are in on at least one or two full programs per week. I realize that it is not always possible for a busy parent to do this, but I would urge you at least to try to be available during these times. Let your child know in advance that if he wants you for any reason—because he is disturbed by something he is watching, because he wants something explained, because he just needs you there with him—you'll certainly come. When and if this does happen, sit down and *listen* to him, trying to understand the concerns of his that have been stirred up.

Perhaps you might also think about the ways in which you can use television as a positive and cementing force within your family. For example, most mothers need a baby sitter at certain times of the day. They need the relief from demands of housekeeping and child rearing, the time to prepare the evening meal, an organizing force to bring children down from the exciting experiences of the day to a more relaxed, comfortable state. Appropriate programs could help to do this *and* provide children with a worthwhile experience. Programs that bring all the members of the household together after supper can be an opportunity for valuable interaction—for example, word games or guessing games in which all ages can participate actively *as a family.*

There is just one more point I would like to make. I believe one hour a day is the maximum amount of time a child up to the age of five or six can spend in front of a television set before he begins to show the signs of depletion and exhaustion that I mentioned earlier. But parents, in particular mothers, must always be on the lookout for the symptoms. Whenever they appear you can be certain that your child has had too much, and you must reduce the television-watching time accordingly.

In attempting to outline some of the problems television causes and in trying to give some ways of coping with them, I am not suggesting that we eliminate television altogether—I certainly am not that much of an ostrich. But I would urge all of us who are parents to take a more active role in this part of our children's lives. We must replace the almost total lack of control that exists today with individual choice, with the freedom to decide upon or to refuse a program. This kind of active participation on the part of the parent, as well as the child, may begin to make television the valuable experience it should be.

*   *   *

In the past few years, there has been more research and far more concern in the area of television programing designed for children. *The Family Guide to Children's Television* is the prime example of a new awareness of the need of parents for information about the television that their children may see. One of the best starting places for a concerned family would be to read this book, and to experiment with the many viewing suggestions it contains. It can be the first step to active involvement in the viewing experiences of our children.

The Family Guide
to Children's Television

Introduction

"WHO IS TALKING TO YOUR CHILDREN?"

The room is half-darkened. In the corner the television shows an animated cartoon of a large animal chasing two smaller animals. Loud music accompanies the chase.

The screen then shows two figures from "The Flintstones" cartoon demonstrating the contents of a box of cereal—"If you put sweet Pebbles in your mouth, you won't have rocks in your head." There is rock music and the animated characters dance around. Next on the screen is a man walking slowly up behind a woman. He catches her by the throat and starts to strangle her. A tense voice urges, "Watch 'The Terror of the Underworld' on Adult Movies tonight at eleven on this station." With an echoing scream the woman fades away. The picture of the animal chase then reappears and a voice says, "Now back to 'Kimba.'"

A young boy sits sprawled on a chair watching the screen. He is chewing gum and looks mesmerized. Suddenly a woman comes into the room. "Good grief, what are you doing sitting in here? I thought you were outside riding your bike. Turn that thing off and go outside; it's a beautiful day."

The boy doesn't move, doesn't seem to have heard her. She goes to the TV and turns it off. He stretches, twists, yawns. "Now go outside," she says firmly. "That's enough TV for now." The boy wanders out of the room, mumbling, "I don't want to go out."

The woman watches him go. Did I do the right thing? she wonders. He wasn't bothering anyone. He had played outside earlier anyway. Maybe he'd have a fight with his brother now.

Parents today have a visitor in their homes. It produces a variety of reactions and can be found in over 95 percent of American households. The visitor is television and it has been here since the 1950s, almost two decades ago. Many adults feel a certain amount of guilt about watching television. They think that it is less worthwhile than reading a book or clearing up the yard. This is partly because of their ambivalence about the programs themselves. While we declare publicly that it is essential to have many regular news and cultural programs on TV, it is much easier to turn the dial to the movie rerun or the comedy hour which is inane but relaxing. Also an incredible deluge of advertising accompanies television programs, coloring our attitudes and speech to such an extent that advertising slogans become national catch-phrases.

Although parents learn to cope with their own feelings about television, they are often confused about their children's viewing attitudes. Most people over twenty-one can remember a time before television took over as the mass entertainer. But for young children and adolescents life without television is as unthinkable as life without electricity or cars or the sky.

Television fascinates many children, often more than radio, records, or books. While parents report that some children are bored by watching and voluntarily seek out other activities, most will sit passively for hours absorbing whatever images move across the screen and the jumble of music, words, programs, and ads that make up a TV soundtrack. According to John Condry, Associate Professor of Human Development and Family Studies at Cornell University:

Our understanding of the impact of this medium has lagged far behind its commercial success. We have only recently become aware of the changes it has brought about in the nature of politics, the entertainment industry, and the dissemination of news. Whether these changes will be, in the long run, good or bad is still to be determined. Yet the changes television brings to these and other areas of American life may prove trivial compared to its potential effect upon the lives of children.*

What can parents do to cope with TV and to help their children live with this new medium? *The Family Guide to Children's Television* incorporates the experience of many parents, from different parts of the country and different ways of life, including those involved with the work of Action for Children's Television (ACT). We welcome your comments, ideas, and suggestions.

HOW MUCH DO YOU KNOW ABOUT CHILDREN'S TELEVISION?

Before you turn to Chapter 1, test your knowledge of children's television with the following quiz. Score yourself. If you get less than 100 percent, read on. There is more you should know about children's TV.

1. *There are more commercials in daytime programs for children than in evening programs for adults.*
   True   False

2. *By the time a child has finished high school, he has spent 11,000 hours in classrooms. How many hours were spent watching television during those years?*
   2,000 hours   10,000 hours   15,000 hours

3. *What percentage of Saturday morning children's programs have at least one example of human violence (according to a recent study)?*
   15 percent   38 percent   71 percent   92 percent

* *Action for Children's Television*, pp. 61–62.

4. *Is there any relationship between televised violence and aggressive behavior in children?*
definitely yes   definitely no   probably yes   probably no

5. *What network runs children's programs with no commercials?*
ABC   CBS   NBC   PBS

6. *The two most commonly advertised products on programs designed for children are (circle two):*
toothpaste   fish   milk   apples   candy
cookies   toys   snack foods   cheese   cereals
vitamin pills   soap   peanut butter   carrots   juice

7. *About what percentage of Saturday network commercial TV programs for children are cartoons?*
75 percent   50 percent   25 percent   10 percent

8. *The hosts of programs and cartoon characters in children's TV shows are forbidden to introduce or present any commercials.*
True   False

9. *The government has set regulations for all advertising that children might see.*
True   False

10. *Match up the following characters with the correct programs:*

Program	Character
A. "Captain Kangaroo"	1. John-Boy
B. "Vision-On"	2. Kukla
C. "Kid Power"	3. Fargo North, Decoder
D. "H.R. Puf'n'Stuf"	4. Tony
E. "ZOOM!"	5. Mr. Spock
F. "Mister Rogers' Neighborhood"	6. Rocky
G. "Children's Film Festival"	7. Mr. Moose
H. "The Waltons"	8. Guest of the Week
I. "Star Trek"	9. Lady Elaine
J. "The Electric Company"	10. Witchy-poo

Answers

1. True
2. 15,000 hours
3. 71 percent
4. definitely yes
5. PBS
6. Any of the following: cereals, snack foods, toys, candy, cookies
7. 75 percent
8. True
9. False
10. "Captain Kangaroo"—Mr. Moose
    "Vision-On"—Tony
    "Kid Power"—Rocky
    "H.R. Puf'n'Stuf"—Witchy-poo
    "ZOOM!"—Guest of the Week
    "Mister Rogers' Neighborhood"—Lady Elaine
    "Children's Film Festival"—Kukla
    "The Waltons"—John-Boy
    "Star Trek"—Mr. Spock
    "The Electric Company"—Fargo North, Decoder

drawing by Rob Chalfen

CHAPTER
1
TO VIEW OR NOT TO VIEW

drawing by Susan

Statistically, children spend more time watching television than in any other single activity except sleep. Television sets in homes with preschool children are on approximately fifty-four hours a week according to viewing figures from A. C. Nielsen. Children under five years of age watch television an average of between twenty-two and twenty-five hours a week, which means three to four hours a day. By the time a child graduates from high school, he will have spent an average of 15,000 hours watching television compared with 11,000 hours in school.

WHAT'S YOUR TOTAL?

Parents who are starting to wonder about television and its effects on their children might like to try checking TV watching for a week by jotting down how many hours their own children watch, or asking their children to do it themselves (see "Children's Workbook," pp. 94–5). Many parents may be surprised to discover how much time their children actually spend in front of the TV. Other parents may find that TV is only one activity within a week that is full of other things to do. And some parents who keep the set on all day as a background to other activities may not consider this as "viewing" in the strict sense of the word. Each family has its own feelings about television and it is important to make sure that you feel comfortable about the kind of viewing that your children do. But first find out.

HOW TO REGULATE TV VIEWING

Parents have different ways of regulating TV viewing in their families. You can choose from a range of parent-tested methods if you decide that your child is watching too much television.

1. No television viewing at all; it is an adult occupation. Some parents of very young children feel that this is an essential rule.
2. Limited number of hours for viewing TV. It could be an hour a day on school days, perhaps more on weekends. Or a total number of hours each week.
3. No viewing until homework or chores are completed, or during specific times. Some parents find it helps to keep the set off during meal times, music practice times, or early morning hours before school.
4. Viewing only during weekends, not during the week.
5. No viewing of commercial television programs, only public (non-commercial) television prgrams.
6. Select programs in advance from television listings and permit the set to be on only at those times.

7. Viewing only in bad weather when children cannot play outside. This is easier in climates with mild winters or in areas where children have adequate play space outside.
8. Unlimited viewing at any time. Parents who choose this method believe that it is all right for the child to decide what he wants to watch without any parental guidance.

Many parents find it helpful to discuss television viewing with older children and to talk to them about the kind of rules that they would find acceptable. Sometimes children appreciate a firm stand on viewing and welcome knowing where the boundaries

are. It is wise to tell your children in advance of any regulations that you set, so that they know what is going to happen. With young children, there may be noisy complaints when you first implement certain rules and turn the set off to comply with the limits.

HOME SITUATION AND TV

The amount of television a child watches often depends on his particular situation at home. A young child alone at home with a parent may start watching television because there is little else provided for him to do. If no older brothers and sisters or friends are around, television may be a substitute. But often a parent can wean his child from the television by providing simple, creative toys or activities for him to become involved in. A morning spent mixing flour and water for play dough will make most children happier than watching the game shows and old movies

which many TV stations run in the early part of the day. For older children, television may be an escape when they are timid about playing with new friends or when they are having a difficult time in a neighborhood situation. Parents can often help by talking to their children about excessive TV watching. They can also set up enjoyable outings or local activities involving neighbors.

Unusual situations, such as moving or receiving unexpected visitors, or times of stress, such as sickness or the extended absence of a parent, may mean that parents have less time to spend with their child and that he is left to watch television. After the normal routine is interrupted for some reason, it is sometimes difficult to stop the temporary increase in viewing when the situation returns to normal. It is important for a child to know that in times of stress and confusion he can turn to his parents for the time and attention that he needs, rather than to the television set.

DON'T ABANDON A CHILD TO THE TV SET!

Leaving a young child alone in a room with a television set is not recommended. The parent then has no idea what the child is watching and is allowing the child to make many viewing decisions that he may not be capable of making. If the child is worried or frightened about something he sees, he has nobody to turn to for comfort. Often young children become addicted to television and suffer "withdrawal symptoms" when the set is removed.

Many parents suggest keeping the television set in a room near the kitchen or some other activity area where they can keep an eye on what their child is watching. Parents can then suggest other activities when a program seems unsuitable or can answer a child's questions about a confusing aspect of program content.

QUESTIONS PARENTS ASK

Question: Children spend all day in school learning. Why can't they be allowed to relax and enjoy TV in the afternoons and weekends?

Answer: They certainly can, but for a child, learning and entertainment are not totally separate. Children learn from everything they see and do. They learn from an outdated animated cartoon, and from a program labeled "educational." Some parents have found that watching certain kinds of TV programs is not relaxing for their children at all, but instead provokes tension and irritability. Pediatricians and others who work with children have noted the same syndrome. Dr. Aletha Huston Stein, writing on "Mass Media and Young Children's Development" in the *Yearbook of the National Society for the Study of Education, 1972,* states:

Children apparently react to media more intensely than adults. More important, they often interpret a plot differently and, as a result, respond emotionally to different aspects of its content.*

Her studies also found that media presentations involving violence, danger, conflict, and tragedy do stimulate immediate emotional reactions. Another study found that children watching an aggressive cartoon exhibited more signs of anxiety than those watching a nonaggressive cartoon.†

It is important for parents to know which programs make their children feel good and which don't. Broadcasters, on the other hand, should assume the responsibility for providing as

* P. 18.
† David L. Lange, Robert K. Baker, and Sandra J. Ball, *Mass Media and Violence:*

varied a range of programs for children as possible, so that the child will have a real choice in what he can watch.

Question: I tried setting some limits on what my children watched but it caused such arguments that I wonder if it's worth it.

Answer: It is hard to set rules in any family. But it is important to realize that young children think that adults control everything in the home and presume that what comes over the television is there with parental approval also. You can show your concern for your children by setting limits, so that they will know how you feel about television. Children often appreciate rules once they know you mean what you say and as long as the rules are applied consistently.

drawing by Michele

CHAPTER

2

WILL IT HURT?
PROFESSIONAL OPINIONS

Many professionals who work with children daily—teachers, pediatricians, child psychiatrists—are aware of the amount of television children watch. Their comments echo the concerns of parents across the country. Although there is no general agreement among experts about whether watching TV is good or bad for children, many are concerned about its effects, both the physical and emotional effects of sitting passively for long periods of time and the emotional effects of the kinds of programs watched. Dr. Richard Granger, Associate Professor of Clinical Pediatrics at the Yale University Child Center, has stated:

We have, as a nation, acted as though no body of knowledge about the developmental needs and pitfalls of childhood existed. If this is so for a society at large, why pick on television in particular? A prime reason is that for a large number of children, television *is* society at large. Through its powerfully combined audio and visual impact delivered directly into the child's home, it is the face of the adult world, the reflection of society.*

* *"Who Is Talking to Our Children?"* p. 8.

In 1971, the American Academy of Pediatrics, representing 12,000 pediatricians in the United States, Canada, and Latin America, wrote to the Federal Communications Commission:

We are naturally concerned with television programing for our children, since this communications medium today affects so significantly the learning and behavioral habits of children. We feel it is essential that commercial broadcasters recognize their responsibility to program for the child audience. . . . We urge that at least half of all prime time be especially constructed with the best interests of children in mind.*

Bernice Miller, Associate Director of the Center for Urban Studies, Harvard University, and one of the founders of the New School, an experimental elementary school for black children, in Roxbury, Massachusetts, has voiced a strong criticism of current children's TV:

One, television is misused. Two, it perpetuates racial prejudice in a racist society. Three, it has a great potential which we have not as yet explored. And four, educators ought to get into the fight, particularly teachers, because if television is ever developed as a learning device it is going to be the teacher who is still going to be in constant contact with the child.†

The National Child Research Center in Washington, D.C., was also critical in its 1971 filing with the FCC:

Television represses children's innate tendencies because it requires passive rather than active involvement, and activity not passivity is necessary for children's full healthful development. . . .

Nursery school teachers know that young children need to learn by doing a variety of things. A good nursery or preschool will provide building blocks, puzzles, vessels to fill and empty, open and shut. There will be materials to mess with like water, play dough, clay, and paint, and dolls and animals for children to spank, wash, dry, dress, soothe, and cuddle. When young children spend a great deal of their time watching television, they lose an irreplaceable opportunity to learn the essential tasks for their age.

* From a submission in response to the FCC public notice about ACT's guidelines for children's programing.
† *Action for Children's Television*, p. 58.

Dorothy Cohen, educator and author, reported that nursery school teachers are noticing a difference in the quality of children's play depending on the amount of television they see.

Teacher feedback in the primary grades shows that they are finding strong resistance among children not only to reading but to exerting any kind of effort. Something is happening to children in their ability to *do*.*

Dr. Lee Salk, in his column in *McCalls* magazine in December, 1972, was more positive about children's television—in moderation.

* *"Who Is Talking to Our Children?"* p. 18.

Too much television is bad for a child—and for that matter, too much of anything is bad for anybody.

I must say that I think that many children are inadvertently forced into bad TV habits by their parents. When a parent wants some time alone or has been overburdened by a curious and enthusiastic child, it is too easy to say, "Why don't you go and watch TV for a while?" Some parents offer extended viewing hours as a reward, others take it away as punishment. And so the importance of television is enhanced.

I do feel, however, that television has some fascinating programs to offer; but as with all other forms of entertainment, it is necessary for a parent to provide guidelines. If children see adults watching indiscriminately for hours, it is hard for them to see why they cannot do the same.

I think that a parent should help a child select programs that are emotionally and intellectually stimulating, and then be firm in limiting viewing to these. It is also far easier to divert a child with an interesting book or hobby than it is to turn off the TV and offer no alternative at all.*

The actual physical dangers of watching television can be more easily pinpointed and prevented. There may be some radia-

* Reprinted from December 1972 issue of *McCalls* magazine, "You and Your Family," by Dr. Lee Salk.

tion from some color TV sets, and manufacturers advise sitting a specific distance from the set in order to avoid any danger. It is best to carefully read the instructions for your new set. The American Optometric Association has studied the effect of TV viewing on the eyes and has prepared a pamphlet, "To View or Not to View,"* which states:

When properly installed and viewed, television is not harmful to the eyes or to vision. There is, normally, much less focus strain involved in viewing television than in doing close work such as reading or sewing. However, close concentration on the television screen over an excessive period of time may result in general fatigue. The AOA suggests that it is better not to sit too close to the screen, and recommends a distance of at least five times the width of the picture.

Their other recommendations include not watching in a completely dark room, not wearing sunglasses when watching, and not placing the TV set where there will be glare or reflections from lights or windows.

drawing by Rob Chalfen

* This pamphlet is available free from the American Optometric Association, 7000 Chippewa St., St. Louis, Missouri 63119.

CHAPTER
3

THE BUSINESS OF BROADCASTING

At present, American television is divided into two major broadcasting outlets. The commercial broadcasters pay for programing costs by accepting commercials from advertisers. Most local commercial broadcasters are affiliated with one of the three major networks—ABC, CBS, and NBC. But any broadcaster may own up to five VHF or seven UHF stations and many of them have formed mini-networks, such as the Westinghouse, Avco, and Meredith Broadcasting Corporations. There are also a few independent stations.

Commercial broadcasters clearly make substantial profits. In 1972 television broadcasting revenues climbed to $3.18 billion, up 15.6 percent from 1971, and pretax profits of $522 million exceeded 1971 profits by 41.9 percent. The profits are distributed unevenly, however, among the 701 stations, the fifteen stations belonging to ABC, CBS, and NBC accounting for $111 million, more than double their profits of the year before.

Noncommercial public television is funded from government and foundation grants and contributions from companies and the community. Local stations are independent but linked voluntarily through the Public Broadcasting Service (PBS), and do not air any commercials.

All broadcasting stations, both radio and television, are licensed by the Federal Communications Commission in Washington, D.C., and must apply for license renewals every three years. (A list of major TV groups is given in the Resource Directory.)

COMMERCIAL TELEVISION

In 1971, the Federal Communications Commission commissioned Dr. Allan Pearce, an economist, to carry out an extensive study of "the economics of children's television programming." Dr. Pearce found:

In the broadcasting business, ratings determine revenue. The bigger a network's audience, the more it can charge for the time it sells to advertisers. From an advertiser's point of view, what matters is the size of the audience watching the program surrounding the commercial minutes. The ratings points, which express the absolute numbers of television homes tuned in to a particular program, are, in effect, the only way broadcasters have yet figured out to price their merchandise, which is the time the public spends watching television. . . .

Audience measurement ratings equate with circulation (or readership) in the print media, with one important economic difference . . . if a newspaper publisher has a newspaper operation that costs $1 million a day, with a daily circulation of one million and advertising revenues of $500,000 daily, he has to sell his newspapers for 50 cents each in order to break even. . . . If a broadcaster has a product —a children's television special, for example—that costs one million to produce and sell at a profit, and he has an audience of a million households, it costs him $1.00 for each household in the audience and he attempts to fix the rates for his commercial minutes accordingly. If the audience for the show increases to two million households, the unit cost becomes only 50 cents, and so on. The broadcasters, like the newspaper or magazine owner, can charge more for his commercial minutes because he is offering a larger audience to the advertisers, but *unlike* his competitors in the print media, the broadcaster's unit costs always fall once break-even point has been reached.*

In his excellent book, *Television: The Business Behind the Box*, Les Brown, now broadcasting editor for the *New York Times* and for many years the leading TV columnist for *Variety* newspaper, describes what has come to be the attitude of commercial networks:

In day-to-day commerce, television is not so much interested in the business of communications as in the business of delivering people to advertisers. People are the merchandise, not the shows. The shows are merely the bait. The consumer, whom the custodians of the medium are pledged to serve, is in fact served up.†

Counter-programing

The average viewer would probably prefer to be offered a choice of programs on different channels at the same time. One station could offer a movie, another a talk show, while a third aired some music or a variety hour. But we all know that movies are usually run at the same time as other movies, that talk shows run against other talk shows, and that all stations run their news programs at the same time. It is no different for children. On Saturday mornings all three commercial networks run children's programs because the majority of available viewers are children.

The pressures of ratings make it essential for a program to attract the largest *share* of the available audience. A network may have five million viewers for its program, but if the total available audience was twenty million and the other two networks attracted seven and a half million each, it failed.

* *The Economics of Children's Television Programming*, pp. 3–4.
† *Television: The Business Behind the Box*, p. 15.

Statistics always show that large numbers of children are watching television in the late afternoon. But the total audience contains far more adults. It is, therefore, better for the network affiliates to attract the largest share of the available audience by putting on adult programs than to lose it by putting on children's shows, even though they may attract a sizable number of children. Sometimes when major stations are running adult shows, local independent stations will counter-program, that is, run low-cost cartoon reruns to attract the large child audience, since they feel that in the late afternoon they cannot compete in attracting the "cream" adult audience.

The only possible change in such pressures is the availability of additional television channels. As more channels become available in different areas, audiences become more specialized. Public television has already shown that quality children's TV programs like "Sesame Street," which are well-produced and entertaining, can attract a reasonably large audience. In areas where there is no public TV, many commercial stations run "Sesame Street" without commercials because the quality of the program will attract a large number of children.

But at present, the pressures of competition are so fierce that no major station will willingly forgo its share of the audience by programing for children in the late afternoon or during the daytime on a regular basis. In the same way, the Saturday morning chase-and-bop cartoons have been shown to attract children from ages two to eleven, a wide range, while a program designed for a specific age range, say six to eleven, would lose some part of that audience and, therefore, get low ratings. Because it is essential, for maximum profits, to claim a maximum audience at all times, programing aimed at children of a specific age is likely to be quickly replaced by cartoons which can attract the broadest span of the available child audience.

PUBLIC TELEVISION

Public television is funded from sources other than advertising revenues based on ratings and has managed to provide a regular daily schedule of television programs designed for children of various ages. In many areas of the country, there are TV programs during the day designed for viewing in the schools as part of a definite curriculum. Public television is usually the only network regularly carrying such programs to the schools and cooperating with educators in this important area.

BROADCASTING: HOW IT WORKS

NETWORKS

Commercial Networks:*   **Non-Commercial Network:**

ABC	CBS	NBC	
5 owned and operated TV stations	5 owned and operated TV stations	5 owned and operated TV stations	Owns NO stations

PROGRAM DISTRIBUTION

To 5 stations and 181 affiliates	To 5 stations and 192 affiliates	To 5 stations and 219 affiliates	Distributes to 245 non-commercial stations

FINANCIAL SUPPORT

Funds raised from advertising sales through:
  a) network commercials and sponsorship, from range of business and companies
  b) local commercials, sponsorship and promotional advertising by local companies
[In 1972 pretax profits for all three networks totaled $522 million.]

Public broadcasting funds come from:
  a) Corporation for Public Broadcasting (CPB) which administers government grants
  b) donations from viewers and major companies
  c) foundation grants
  d) annual TV auctions
  e) corporate underwriting
[Nonprofit]

PRODUCTION OF PROGRAMS

Major networks and station groups, as well as local stations, produce program series, specials, and news programs or commission independent producers to make shows.

Local stations produce all programs, some of which are aired nationally.

Programs and series are purchased from independent sources or after being shown on the air, either in USA or other countries.

---

  * There are also several major station groups such as Westinghouse and Metromedia which own up to seven TV stations. No broadcaster may own more than five VHF stations, but a broadcaster may own up to seven UHF stations. A recent FCC Policy Statement also stressed that broadcasters who own more than three stations in the top fifty markets must show special reasons why they should own more. This statement, an effort to encourage diversity of ownership, has so far had little effect.

It might be interesting to check the weekly schedule of programs in your area to see which stations provide children's programs, when they air them, and if they produce any locally. In most areas, the public TV station is alone in providing quality programs for children on a regular basis.

CABLE TELEVISION

The present narrow system of limited channel broadcasting may change significantly over the next few years as more and more communities become involved in cable television. Cable is simply a method of bringing a television signal into the home by means of an underground cable rather than over the air from a transmitter. It can provide a greater number of stations and usually an improved quality of reception. Cable TV revenues come from subscriber fees, multiple outlet charges, installation and reconnect charges, and advertising, which is allowed on locally originated programs.

Local communities and state organizations are now looking into cable television as a possible way to provide some constructive alternatives for children's programs. (See the Resource Directory, pp. 161–62, for organizations and publications that can provide the details of community involvement in cable television.)

The following is *Broadcasting* magazine's "Short Course in Cable":

There are 3,100 operating cable systems in the U.S., serving 5,770 communities. Another 2,500 systems are approved but not built. Pennsylvania has the most systems (300) and California the most subscribers (1.2 million). Operating systems currently reach about 8.1 million subscribers, perhaps 25.92 million people—12.5% of the nation's TV households. The average cable system has 2,400 subscribers. The largest (Cox Cable's, in San Diego) has over 75,000. Some have fewer than 100. Teleprompter is the largest multiple system operator (MSO), with more than one million subscribers. Most systems offer between eight and 12 channels. Systems in the top 100 markets will be required to have 20-channel capacity by 1977; those constructed after March 1972 must do so now. Monthly subscriber fees average $5.40, although many firms are now seeking rate increases. Installation fees range from nothing to $100; the average is $15. Costs of laying cable range from $4,000 per mile in rural areas to $75,000 in the largest cities. The average system has between 100 and 200 miles of cable. Nearly 600 systems now originate programing in their own studios, the average for 12 hours weekly. Equipment costs range from $25,000 for a small black-and-white operation to $200,000 for a color studio. Over 300 systems accept advertising on their local-origination channels, with rates frm $5 to $200 per minute. Pay cable is on approximately 50 systems and reaches 50,000 subscribers. Other media interests have ownership holdings in approximately 74% of all cable firms. . . .*

To date, cable has done little more than provide better reception for people in those areas where over-the-air reception is poor. That means that cable TV can bring you "The Lucy Show" with a clearer picture. But according to studies and cable TV operators, the *possibilities* for cable TV are boundless.

By the end of the decade a cable television system will be in existence which covers 40 to 60 per cent of all American television homes; which provides in a majority of instances a capacity of twenty channels and in many instances a capacity of forty channels or more; which possesses a limited capacity for return signals from the home receiver back to the point of transmission; and which will be extensively interconnected, most probably by satellite.

This was one of the general conclusions in *On the Cable*, the report of the Sloan Commission on Cable Communications, published in 1971.†

Those involved in cable television promise exciting diversity in its future. In upper New York City today, Telepromoter is offering eighteen channels, including continuous AP news wires in Spanish and English, stock market quotations, weather reports, and a few public access programs. During the epic Fischer-

---

* *Broadcasting*, April 22, 1974.

† Pp. 173–174. This study was commissioned by the Alfred P. Sloan Foundation, New York.

Spassky chess matches, cable provided ten hours of coverage daily for its New York audience.

Ben Bagdikian makes another forecast for cable television:

There will be profound social consequences to the choices made in the new media. . . . Increased numbers of vivid channels into the home will make demagoguery and public deception more effective than ever before. The power to record instant reactions to presentations, and thus conduct an accurately counted poll, could produce irreversible reactions to manipulated public information.*

Whether either or both these predictions prove true is still a matter for conjecture. It is clear that the multiplicity of television channels can provide either the repetitive diversity of radio or a broader and more public-service-oriented choice for the viewer.

Because cable TV reaches a much smaller audience and pinpoints its locality, its chief advantage is that it will be able to program to the special needs of the community and especially to its children. According to current FCC regulations, three channels on the cable must be made available to the community for 1) municipal programing, 2) educational needs, and 3) community access.

It is up to citizens of communities to see that the holder of the cable franchise fulfills his obligations and makes time and facilities available for children's programing. Since cable reaches limited audiences, it could provide programs for special age groups, for deaf children, for hospitalized children, for disturbed children, and could even provide far more opportunities for children to make programs themselves.

BROADCASTING AND THE INDIVIDUAL

The Communications Act of 1934 was expressly designed to stress the importance of considering the public's needs in broad-

---

* Ben H. Bagdikian, *The Information Machines: Their Impact on Men and the Media* (New York: Harper & Row, 1971).

casting decisions. Stations must be operated "in the public interest, convenience and necessity," and while those three words may be interpreted in many ways, it is clear that the spirit of the Act is to ensure that broadcasting is responsive to the needs of the community and the viewer.

It is most important that citizens recognize their responsibility in this area. Each individual can have a voice in expressing ideas and opinions to a local broadcaster, and groups of individuals representing major segments of a community have a clear legal right to insist that local broadcasting reflect their interests and viewpoints.

Until recently there was little awareness of the citizen's rights in broadcasting, and most broadcasters did little to inform the public of them. However, in recent years pressure from many groups concerned about the lack of representation of various ideas and philosophies has begun to bring about some change in television today. In the sensitive area of broadcasting for children, it is even more vital that issues such as racism, sexism, and discrimination be carefully examined, and that broadcasters be always aware that programs must be designed to meet the needs of the wide variety of children in the viewing audience.

HOW CHILDREN'S PROGRAMS ARE MADE

Until 1970, no network and few local commercial stations had any qualified individuals responsible for children's programs. The daytime program producer took charge of the few children's shows that were scattered among the quiz shows, soap operas, and games. In January 1970, ACT representatives met in New York with several CBS TV officials, and discussed with them the issue of responsibility for children's programs, among other things. This meeting was reported in the *New York Times* and shortly afterward all three commercial TV networks appointed vice-presidents for children's programing. A few local stations also appointed special producers for children's programs. However, since the new appointments were not accompanied with adequate funding or commitment of facilities for producing and planning children's programs, the vice-presidents became public relations figureheads for network efforts to upgrade programing. Even now, there is no permanent children's television unit in any commercial network and no long-term planning for children's programing over the next few years. Network children's programs are still Saturday morning cartoons with a stereotyped format, produced mainly by slick cartoon animation companies in Los Angeles.

In a few areas, responsible broadcasters have initiated locally produced children's programs that are creative and of high quality, geared to the needs of the community. Some examples are the Post-Newsweek stations in Washington, D.C., and Florida, WCVB in Boston, and WPIX in New York. But CBS is the only commercial TV network that runs a one-hour preschool program —"Captain Kangaroo"—Monday through Friday.

A creative, constructive TV series needs time for research and preparation, commitment of creativity and originality, and a clear awareness that the measure of the program's success is its ability to meet the needs of children. In network television, the pressures to attract high ratings make it undesirable for producers to design experimental programs on a wide variety of diverse subjects for children. Instead, most network executives have decided that children's programs must be animated cartoons.

A brief summary of the different program production methods in three different kinds of children's series will give you some idea of how such decisions are made.

Network Animated Cartoons

On Saturday mornings, networks air their children's program schedules. In the 1973–1974 season, this meant some twenty-five animated cartoon series. Most of the series were produced in the Los Angeles area by large animation companies, such as Hanna-Barbera, and use the same artists, voices, and music. Consequently, there is a great similarity among the programs.

Decisions about children's program series are made by network executives in the spring. Since it is generally accepted at network level that animated cartoons attract the largest audience of children aged two to eleven, there has been little change in the format for the Saturday morning line-up for several years. Network executives do not plan a varied five-hour span of programing for children from 8:00 A.M. to 1:00 P.M., but simply invite animation companies to submit ideas to fill that time with cartoons. These ideas, in the form of story outlines or drawings on story boards, are presented to the network executives, who then decide what to order. Usually it is thirteen or twenty-six weeks of a series, with an agreement about the number of reruns and airings. There is little discussion of the value of such programs or the lack of diversity that results from the three networks scheduling fifteen hours of animated cartoons on Saturday morning. There is little examination of the implications of the story lines, the characters, or the settings in terms of their impact on children. There is no testing or research of any kind of program segments or pilot programs on groups of children or parents. The networks have few standards or guidelines for the programing, and the animation companies certainly don't expect to be involved in research or content examination at any point.

SATURDAY MORNING NETWORK PROGRAMS
1974–1975 SCHEDULE

^ Animated Cartoon

	ABC	CBS	NBC
8:00	Yogi and His Friends^	Speed Buggy^	Addams Family^
8:30	Bugs Bunny^	Scooby Doo, Where Are You?^	Chopper Bunch^
9:00	Kung Phooey^	Jeannie^	Emergency + 4^
9:30	The New Adventures of Gilligan^	Partridge Family: 2200 A.D.^ _ _ _ _ _ In the News (8 2-minute segments on hour and half-hour from 8 to noon)	Run, Joe, Run^
10:00	Devlin^	Valley of the Dinosaurs^	Land of the Lost^
10:30	Krog: 70,000 B.C.^	Shazam!^	Sigmund and the Sea Monsters
11:00	Super Friends^	Harlem Globetrotters Popcorn Machine^	The Pink Panther Show^
11:30		Hudson Bros. Razzle Dazzle Comedy Show	Star Trek^
12:00	These Are the Days	U.S. of Archie^	Jetsons^
12:30	American Bandstand	Fat Albert and the Cosby Kids^	GO!
1:00		CBS Children's Film Festival	
1:30			

Most of the cartoons on television now use a form of limited animation, where only the eyes and mouths of the characters move. This is much less expensive and quicker to produce than the full animation used in older cartoons. Music, dialogue, and sound effects are plugged in last rather than carefully synchronized. Worst of all is the added artificial laugh track, which can hardly modify the violence, explosions, and confusion in these cartoons. The chief concern of the animation companies seems to be to produce their product in the cheapest and easiest way.

All the network asks of the animator is that he provide the required amount of cartoon material for airing at the right time with the right holes for commercials. The network's main concern is to attract advertising to the Saturday morning cartoons in order to make its profits. All the animator asks of the network is to be paid.

The local broadcaster can decide whether or not to air a network program, or whether to replace it with a local program. He can also insert local commercials. According to the broadcasting regulations, it is the local broadcaster who is responsible for what is aired on his stations, and he should be aware of the programs he shows. But few broadcasters preview or even watch the networks' animated cartoon series.

Educational Programs

Most educational programs for children have been designed in a totally different way even though they too use a certain amount of animation and cartoon formats. "Sesame Street," a one-hour daily program designed to teach preschool children the alphabet and numbers, uses animation in its letter and number segments. "The Electric Company," a half-hour daily program designed to teach older children how to read, uses animation and computer-designed graphics to teach phonics, letter combinations, and specific words. Both series are produced by the Children's Television Workshop in New York City, a nonprofit corporation.

A great deal of time was spent prior to production in discussing the goals and aims of both of these series. Many meetings and conferences were held with child development experts, parents, researchers, teachers, and others to examine what was essential and what should be omitted in the content of the programs. Almost a year was spent in research and preparation before the first program of "Sesame Street" went on the air. This meant that the Children's Television Workshop had to spend part of its grant to support itself and its staff while the preparation part of the program was taking place. But it recognized that this was vital for the success of the program and repeated the process with "The Electric Company."

After the basic content was decided upon, the elements of the material were broken into segments and given to writers, designers, animators, and graphic artists. Each tried to devise the best way to present the educational idea successfully on television. The work of the producer was to segment the work successfully; the work of the director was to translate the creative work of the individual segments into a cohesive whole. Since both "Sesame Street" and "The Electric Company" are videotaped, much of the programs' appeal lies in judicious and accurate editing of the segments into programs.

In contrast to network attitudes toward their animated cartoons, the Children's Television Workshop is actively interested in every portion of its programs before they go on the air. Segments are carefully screened, examined, and viewed by experts and by children to see if the educational aims are achieved. While the program is being aired in schools, researchers check viewing reactions, teachers' opinions, and children's comments. The Children's Television Workshop has a special viewing room set up for showing children segments and whole programs in order to research the effects of the series on a selected audience.

Several major studies have been carried out by the Children's Television Workshop in order to judge the teaching effectiveness of the program, and to try to find out what children have learned from the series, especially those from inner-city or low-income areas. In recent years, non-English-speaking characters have been integrated into the "Sesame Street" cast and there has been an increase in the use of Spanish within the series.

The Children's Television Workshop designs its programs to

help and encourage children to learn, and it is deeply concerned with its responsibility to the viewing audience.

Participatory Television

One of the few television series that encourages active participation by children is "ZOOM!" a weekly half-hour program produced by WGBH-TV, Boston, and aired nationally on public television.

"ZOOM!" is designed to appeal to children aged six to twelve, and all the material on the program is sent in by the audience. The stories, plays, jokes, riddles, games, and tongue-twisters submitted are performed on the program by a group of seven children, chosen as being representative of the audience. The cast changes every twenty-six weeks, in order to give as broad a range of children as possible a chance to appear on the show.

The program also includes filmed segments of children doing interesting things in other parts of the country, such as a girl rodeo rider, a boy baking bread, two boys who catch fish and bake them in mud, a twelve-year-old fiddler from Appalachia, and a blind boy who designed a wooden spin-top game.

In January 1974 over 25,000 letters a week were flooding into the station with suggestions and material for the series. Initially sorted by volunteers, the poems, plays, jokes, and ideas are then sent to the program's staff and cast. They jointly agree on what they like and think will work, and then plan the details of rehearsing plays, reading jokes, and the other aspects of the show. The seven cast members contribute their own ideas and make suggestions about ways of presenting other children's material. Presentations of games and discussions in the studio are unscripted and videotaped live.

Only at the final stage of fitting the material into a half-hour show, with the technical details of editing film and videotape, timing segments, and adding music, is there a total adult involvement. Otherwise, the program is wholly created and produced by children's ideas and contributions.

The viewing audience's criticisms and comments are carefully read by the program staff, and are often adopted in future programs. "ZOOM!" is very concerned with the needs of its viewing audience and has an unusual and immediate gauge for measuring its effectiveness in this mail response.

WHAT HAPPENS IN OTHER COUNTRIES?

A survey of children's TV in sixteen countries (Austria, Australia, Canada, Denmark, Finland, France, Britain, Ireland, Italy, Japan, the Netherlands, Norway, Sweden, Switzerland, the United States, and West Germany) found that in 1971 the United States was the only major country where television networks did not carry weekday afternoon programs for children. The other findings of the study were:

- • • America allows more advertising on children's programs than any other country surveyed.
- • • Only four nations allow advertising on children's programs on some channels: the United States, England, Japan, and Canada.
- • • While American programs often span a two- to twelve-year-old age range, children's TV in other countries tends to be designated for more specific age groups.

It is worth noting that just to the north, Canada is providing an interesting range of programs for children on a regular basis. Many Canadian parents have joined ACT or formed local organizations concerned with children's TV because they are critical of programs and advertising beamed across the border from the United States.

In April, 1974, the Canadian Radio-Television Commission (the Canadian equivalent of the FCC) issued a 150-page report on license renewal applications. The report stated that the CRTC demanded that there be no advertising to children on any Canadian Broadcasting Corporation network or stations, or on any publicly owned radio or television stations, as one of the conditions for license renewal. The ban on ads to children would come into effect on January 1, 1975.

Canadian TV stations, both public and private, have stopped advertising to preschool children since January 1, 1974, and have adopted a voluntary code of restraint in advertising to children generally.

The CRTC report needs approval by the Canadian Parliament before it can be implemented. At present, CBC is supported mainly by government funds, as public television is in America, but it also receives some two million dollars annually from sponsors of children's programs who advertise to children.

Children's television in Canada comes from several production centers. French language programs are produced in Montreal by Radio-Canada, and include "Nik et Pik," a series of the delightful adventures of two puppet mice traveling around the world, "Sol et Gobelet," a series about two clowns, "Bobino," a daily program now in its seventeenth season, and Franfrelouche," a series linked by a puppet-doll who gets involved with familiar fairy stories and changes them around.

In Toronto, CBC provides nineteen hours of children's TV each week, including "Mr. Dress Up" and "Friendly Giant" for preschool children and "The Fit-Stop," an exercise and health program for older children. CBC also produces special segments about children and situations in various parts of Canada which are inserted into "Sesame Street" programs to give them a more Canadian outlook.

Television in the United States is very different from television in other countries. Many have only one or two channels, which are not on all day long. In those where advertising is allowed, it is strictly controlled in length and when it can be aired. The intensive pressures of ratings and competitive programing are almost unknown outside of the United States. But as other countries expand their hours of broadcasting and the number of channels, and begin to depend more on commercial support, they may have to face the same problems America does today.

MINUTES OF ADVERTISING PER HOUR DURING CHILDREN'S PROGRAMING HOURS IN CANADA, JAPAN, UNITED STATES, AND ENGLAND, 1974

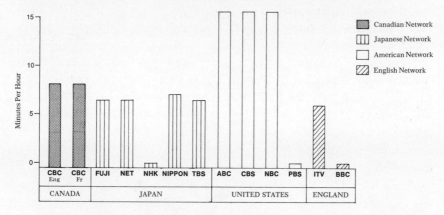

SOURCE: Adapted from Lillian Ambrosine and David Fleiss, *An International Comparison of Children Television Programming*. England was added and Canada adjusted.

Prix Jeunesse

The Prix Jeunesse (Youth Prize) is an international television award given to outstanding television productions for children and young people. The Prix Jeunesse Foundation was established in 1964 by the Free State of Bavaria, the city of Munich, and the Bavarian Broadcasting Corporation to promote programs for the young and to award prizes for the best productions. It aims to be both a competition and a forum for communication and exchange of information, and for improvement of production standards. A conference is held every two years in Munich, Germany, under the auspices of the European Broadcasting Union and UNESCO. The participants select the prize-winning programs. Most of the participants are European, Scandinavian, Canadian, Japanese, or Australian, although many countries with limited television resources also attend. Very few Americans ever participate or submit programs; the conference is given little publicity in the United States.

In 1972, the outstanding film in the children's program category was "Vision-On," a half-hour weekly series produced by the BBC in England, and designed for both deaf and hearing children. This program is shown on some American television stations and is syndicated by Time-Life, Inc.

Although American programs are rarely even shown at Prix Jeunesse meetings, in the last two or three years, several noncommercial children's programs—"ZOOM!", "Sesame Street," "The Electric Company," "Carroscelendas"—have been shown and well received.

drawing by Susan

CHAPTER

4

GUIDELINES TO PROGRAMS

What kind of television programs are there for children to watch? What kind of criteria can we adopt in judging programs? Is there any kind of supervision independently given to children's television? Can parents help their children to develop selectivity in program decisions?

First, there is *no* independent group or agency which, in any way, supervises children's TV programing. The broadcaster alone makes the decision of whether or not to air a certain program designed for children. There are no official standards or guidelines for the quality or quantity of programs shown to children.

Second, since the list of television programs shown to children changes so rapidly, it is a good idea to regularly check the TV page in your local paper to see what is on. Public TV stations often publish their own program guides.

PROGRAM GUIDE FOR PARENTS

The National Association for Better Broadcasting (P.O. Box 130, Topanga, California, 90290) publishes an annual guide to "Family Viewing," which critically reviews television programs. The 1974 guide is reprinted at the end of this book.

Since parents can help a child by guiding him to watch a variety of programs, it is important to know what programs are being shown and what kinds they are.

Parents need to be especially careful about programing in the late afternoon and early evening. The networks run soap operas or movies and local commercial stations run old cartoons, reruns of adult series and game shows, or old movies. Few commercial stations run special children's programs. Only noncommercial public television provides programs designed for children at that time of day.

WHAT PARENTS CAN DO

Parents can be a great help in guiding their children's viewing habits. It is best to sit down with your child and watch some programs together, so that you can make your own judgments while you watch. It is worth watching more than one program of a series because they will often differ greatly.

While you watch, you can:

· · · Decide how your child reacts to what is happening on the screen. Children are different and their reactions to television programs are different. Some children are easily excited or disturbed, others respond little but talk about what they have seen later. Some children react differently when they are tired or hungry. Others react differently if they are viewing with friends or alone.
· · · Try to find out how your child feels about what he is watching and explain to him your feelings. If you object strongly to a program showing killing and shooting, you might explain to him why you feel this way and why you don't want him to watch it.

If you enjoy a particular program, you might talk to him about why you like it and what he might like in it.

· · · Help a young child who might be confused or frightened by events on the screen. So much of television is fragmented that even within children's programing there are announcements and commercials that have no part in a child's life. During one Saturday morning cartoon, there was a sudden newscast showing three jet planes that some hijackers had just blown up. The film of the burning planes and the worried faces of those involved was most disturbing to the children watching, but the mother with them was able to explain the event and to attempt to put it in perspective for them.

· · · Encourage older children to be much more aware of what is happening on the screen. You can help to develop their critical abilities by discussing programs. One teacher gives her class an assignment of watching a program that they usually watch. She then videotapes the program and the following day shows it to them again. She encourages critical discussion about why it was made, what the characters are trying to do, what the purpose of the program is, and for whom it was designed.

• • • Talk about what is on television. One important aspect of television is its ability to bring topics and issues into the home for family discussion. It is helpful for children to learn where you stand on issues such as integration, long hair, or drug use. When parents watch TV with their children, they can make clear their feelings and beliefs on many issues, as well as listen to their child's view.

• • • Always be aware of your importance in expressing opinions about television to children. Researchers have found that children are much influenced, in responding to programs, by the reactions of others viewing with them.*

GENERAL GUIDELINES

Parents often say: "Tell me the good programs and the bad programs, and I'll know what to avoid and what to watch." Unfortunately, it is difficult to say what is clearly good or bad about television programs, because watching TV is unlike being exposed to any other media.

If you decide to take your child to the movies, you choose a particular movie he would enjoy based on your knowledge of it, reviews, or comments from friends. Then he goes to see it once for a few hours, and that's it.

Television is different. Its impact is cumulative. Your child is not going to see one particular program once in his life, or even

* "The Electric Company In-School Utilization Study: The 1971–72 School and Teacher Surveys" was carried out for Children's Television Workshop by the Center for the Study of Education, Institute for Social Research of Florida State University, in conjunction with the Statistics Research Division of the Research Triangle Institute. Findings revealed that involvement in the series was encouraged by discussion before, during, or after viewing. More than 60 percent of the teachers said that discussion *during* the viewing time was helpful. Over 90 percent considered it helpful to hold discussions of the program immediately afterward.

twice. If you have a TV in your home, he is probably going to see a program series daily, or weekly, over months and years.

The National Association for Better Broadcasting has established the following standards for evaluating television programs:

STANDARD	DESIRABLE—IF	UNDESIRABLE—IF
1. Does it appeal to the audience for whom intended?	It gives information and/ or entertainment related to real life situations or interests.	Dull, boring, not related to experience or interests; exaggerated beyond believability.
2. Does it meet people's needs for entertainment and action?	Wholesome adventure, humor, fantasy, suspense.	Unnecessary morbid emphasis on cruelty and violence; loud, crude, or vulgar.
3. Does it add to one's understanding and appreciation of himself, others, the world?	Sincere; constructive; informative; balanced picture of life; encourages decent human relations; fair to races, nations, religions, labor and management.	One-sided propaganda; arouses prejudice; plays on emotions and lack of knowledge.
4. Does it encourage worthwhile ideals, values, and beliefs? (family life, etc.)	Upholds acceptable standards of behavior; promotes democratic and spiritual values, respect for law, decency, service.	Glamorizes crime, indecency, intolerance, greed, cruelty; encourages bad material success, personal taste, false standards of vanity, intemperance, immorality.
5. Does the program stimulate constructive activities?	Promotes interests, skills, hobbies; encourages desire to learn more, to do something constructive, to be creative, to solve problems, to work and to live with others.	Details of theft, robbery, smuggling and other crime; if problems are solved by brute force, or if situations are resolved by chance rather than by logical story development.
6. Does it have artistic qualities?	Skillful production as to music, script, acting, direction, art work, sets, sound effects, photography.	Poorly done job; confusing; hard to follow; action too fast, too slow; sound too loud, too low.

STANDARD	DESIRABLE—IF	UNDESIRABLE—IF
7. Is the commercial acceptable?	Presented with courtesy and good taste, reasonably brief, in harmony with content and sound volume of program; delivered by announcer.	Too loud, too many, deceptive; poor taste in content and treatment.

ADDITIONAL STANDARDS APPLIED SPECIFICALLY TO CHILDREN'S PROGRAMS:

1. Crime is *never suitable* as a major theme of a program for children.
2. There should be immediate resolution of suspense, and the program should avoid undue stress on fear.
3. A clear differentiation should be made between fantasy and fact.

The only consistent guideline we have developed from talking to parents around the country is that any children's program on noncommercial public television is fine. Otherwise, take care! One father said, "When my children watch public television on Saturday morning, I know it's not doing them any harm. But when I know they're looking at that other cartoon stuff, with all those commercials, I really feel concerned."

You may decide that one program you happen to see your child watching is terrible. It may be very violent, pointless, and in your opinion unhealthy. So you turn off the set. But if that program is in a series that is on every day, you will have to ban it every day. If it is syndicated, that same program may return to the air at another time on another station. Your child may start watching it by accident, especially if it is aired in the hours when children are usually watching TV.

Parents should also be aware that some program series change from year to year. They may remember "Lassie," for example, as the tame adventures of a boy and his dog. The original episodes were realistic adventures in a pattern of developing human relationships. But the pressure to attract a larger segment of the audience resulted in more violent incidents, known to frighten children, being written into the script and becoming a regular feature of the program. Parents who think their children might be upset by these should check which "Lassie" series they are watching.

Because of the sheer quantity of television programing, it is virtually impossible for an adult to supervise every single moment of a child's viewing, especially when the child is of school age. Unless you spend every moment with your child when he is watching TV, you will have to make some general rules about watching. And even if you did sit by your child all the time, you would have no idea what kind of programing would come up, or what kinds of promotions for adult shows, commercials, or public service announcements would interrupt the program.

In view of the cumulative effect of TV watching, we should adopt the same approach to television programing for our children that we do to our schools. We are concerned that the schools to which we send our children follow a general trend of education and methods acceptable to us. We don't expect one particular lesson to teach everything, nor do we expect every teacher to be perfect. But we hope that the cumulative effect of the days our children spend in school will encourage them to learn and to appreciate knowledge for its own sake.

Since we know that children spend more time with television than they do in schools, we have every right to expect and demand that the TV programs designed for our children by broadcasters aim for the highest ideals with the most creativity and attractiveness possible.

RANGE OF PROGRAMS

Ideally, in meeting the needs of the different aspects of the child audience, the broadcaster should present as broad a range of programs as he possibly can. Children should be able to watch dramas, documentaries, adventure films, comedy series, and cartoons, and decide from these experiences what they like. It is essential that a choice of programing alternatives be offered, no matter how high or low the ratings.

Unfortunately, commercial television today is concerned mainly with ratings figures and audience-share statistics, so that networks want a program that will attract the largest portion of the available child audience all the time. Since animated cartoons can be watched by two-year-olds, five-year-olds, seven-year-olds, and older children too, most of the programs for children on commercial television are animated cartoons. Fairy stories are animated, adult drama series are animated, comedy series are animated. On Saturday morning network shows, often the only live people are in the commercials.

While there is nothing sinful about animation, it is sad to think that our children are watching nothing else. Television's dramatic and powerful effect is its ability to transport us to different places, and to be a window on the world. If our children see nothing but pint-sized animated figures on the screen, they have no chance to experience the wide range of programing that could be available to them. They have no exposure to a story acted by human beings, to films from other parts of the world, or to unusual and experimental uses of television. Their horizon is limited to stock story lines, stereotype animation, and a repetitive format. They are being deprived of artistic alternatives.

Ironically, when a commercial network does invest in a series that is not a stereotyped animated cartoon, it usually airs it at a time when few children are watching. For example in the 1973–1974 season, an interesting documentary program called "GO!" was aired at 12:30 P.M. on NBC-TV, running against "Fat Albert and the Cosby Kids," an excellent animated series on CBS-TV hosted by Bill Cosby. CBS followed Bill Cosby with an outstanding selection of children's films from around the world called the "CBS Children's Film Festival," which ran from 1:00 to 2:00 P.M. ACT's experience has been that most children who watch TV in the morning are usually away from the set by that time. In fact, this experience has led us to encourage parents to try to take their children out in the morning and bring them back around noon, when the networks will be airing their better quality programs.

ADULT PROGRAMS AT CHILDREN'S HOURS

You may find it virtually hopeless to even look for a "balanced diet" of programing for your child to watch. Apart from public television, which some areas do not receive, there is no regular diet of programs designed for children.

In most other countries in the Western world, it is recognized that the late afternoon–early evening is the time when a parent is most busy, preparing the evening meal and coping with end-of-the-day tiredness. American broadcasters also are certainly not unaware that many children watch TV between 3:00 and 6:00 P.M., for they often put ads directed to children at these times. Yet only one network, ABC-TV, runs an "After-School Special" at 4:30 P.M. every two weeks designed specially for children and worth watching. While broadcasters in other countries program their children's television shows almost exclusively

during that time, concerned American parents can rarely find any program on the air that they would be happy for their children to watch.

The choice will be between reruns of old movies, game shows, reruns of old adult series or of even older cartoons, which often were dropped from the networks because of protests before they were put into syndication.

Most of the programs on the air in the late afternoon were originally produced for an adult audience. They were first shown in the evening as adult shows. Now, according to the reasoning of TV station program managers, the passage of time has made them suitable for children.

Let us look at a case history, "Bewitched" began some years ago with the usual new-season bally-hoo as an evening series about a woman living in the twentieth century, attractive, personable, and modern, who happened to be a witch. The series is based on the humorous, unusual, and unlikely situations in which she finds herself when she uses her witchcraft to solve problems. In 1972 the series was aired by ABC at 11:00 A.M. as a children's Saturday morning program. It is also in syndication and has been aired in the late afternoon shows which have a large child audience. Further, an animated cartoon series based on the program, "Sabrina, the Teenage Witch," was run by CBS on its Saturday morning children's programing schedule for 1972–1973.

Other adult series sometimes follow the same pattern. Some have humor, some adventure, some violence. The essential point for parents to remember is that none of these series was designed with children in mind. The programs were all planned for an adult audience, to appeal to mass tastes, and to be shown in the evening hours.

Death, Killing, and Violence

While the effects of violence in children's TV are considered in Chapter 5 in relation to children's programs, it is also important to examine the effects in relation to adult programs a child might see.

Dr. John E. Schowalter, Director of Training, Child Psychiatry Unit, and Association Professor of Pediatrics and Psychiatry, Yale School of Medicine, has stated: "It is clear that the children most at risk of being harmed by inappropriate programing are those under the age of five or six," but "I have also been consulted by older children whose anxieties or phobias were intertwined with the frightening TV shows that they have seen."*

Some broadcasters allege that parents are shielding children from reality when they attack programs that glorify violence and depict killing. In fact, they suggest that it is a healthy educational process for children to be exposed to such incidents, preparing them for adulthood. It is up to each parent to determine whether programs are "educational" or "frightening" for his child.

You should carefully examine adult programs that contain violence or killing before you decide whether you want your child to watch them. News programs, which often contain real life violence, should be considered in the same way, since they can confuse and upset a young child. Also it is often a great help for a child to watch the news with adults, who can explain what is going on.

SOCIAL RELATIONSHIPS ON PROGRAMS

The types of characters on a program and their relationships with each other are often an indication of whether or not the program is constructive. Many shows are built around a simple conflict situation, which is resolved in the last two minutes.

The major problem in almost all shows is the existence of a power differential. There is somebody who is stronger or bigger or meaner or smarter than somebody else. The pattern of the program and the conflict presented is how to redress or diminish or eliminate that differential. This is a real problem for children, and for adults too. What is striking is the limited range of solutions proposed. You can use magic or cunning or cheating. It is recognized immediately that the hero-figure must be suc-

* *"Who Is Talking to Our Children?"* p. 11.

cessful at the end. No problems are without solutions. But rarely do characters use thoughtfulness, cooperation, or reason to solve them.

Many of the family situation series have little relation to the real life problems of growing children. Family relationships are almost always simplistic stereotypes. Children certainly learn character traits from such series, but rarely ones adaptable to the realities of conflict and disharmony which sometimes occur in real families. One of the entries in the diary of the young man who shot Governor Wallace in 1972 expressed the wish that his family "could be like those happy families on television." Do children understand that no families are like those "ideal" families on television?

In judging social relationships on television programs, parents must decide if they are ones they would be happy to see their children imitate and admire. If not, it may be simpler to stop your children from watching such programs than to argue constantly about values with which you do not agree.

REALITY AND FANTASY

Professionals who work with young children stress that one of the most important lessons a young child must learn is to distinguish between reality and fantasy. Dr. Albert Solnit, Sterling Professor of Pediatrics and Psychiatry and Director of the Yale Child Study Center, has said:

Children under the age of six are more vulnerable to being confused because their sense of reality, their ability to use logic, their ability to use what we call orderly causal thinking is not as available to them developmentally until they are about six or seven. Under six or seven and especially under the age of four, the very strong built-in capacity for explaining things by magical thinking, by the sense of the power of magical feeling, will make them more vulnerable to such confusion.*

* "*Who Is Talking to Our Children?*" p. 30.

When young children meet fantasy in books, they are usually with a sympathetic adult, who is reading to them. If the fantasy becomes too frightening or confusing, the child can stop the adult and ask questions, or simply cuddle up close and enjoy "being scared." The child knows that he can control the situation. Since young children generally cannot read fluently, the hobgoblins and giants of fairy stories come to them through the intermediary of an adult, until they are school age and old enough to handle them.

But with television, this is not the case. The child has no control over the program on the screen in front of him and he cannot stop it at a scary point and ask a question. For many children, television is the real world. When one nursery school teacher asked a young child, "Are Batman and Robin real or pretend?" he replied firmly, "Oh no, they're really real." There would seem to be only harm and no benefit in allowing children to watch programs that upset and confuse them.

Children are often left to cope with a bewildering quantity of confusing information even during commercial breaks. In a pilot study, a TV commercial for a children's game called "The Secret of the Missing Mummy" was shown to a group of preschool children, followed by a few simple questions about what the commercial showed. Many of the young children were very disturbed by the commercial because they assumed that it referred to their own mothers who were missing. When asked why the Mummy was missing, one child replied, "Because she is making peanut butter and jelly sandwiches." Parents can help young children by sitting and watching with them, explaining things, and being ready to answer questions. Older brothers and sisters can sometimes also be helpful in this area.

SEXISM

Programs designed for children echo the same misconceptions of sexism and stereotyping of roles according to sex as those designed for adults. The misconceptions are carried over into the commercials designed for children. In an analysis of commercials directed to children on a Saturday morning in 1972, Dr. F. Earle Barcus of Boston University found that there was a cultural sex bias. Forty-nine commercials contained males only while sixteen contained females only. Characters in toy ads were usually identified by sex roles, girls playing with dolls and boys with cars. Since children will have seen 350,000 commercials and 15,000 hours of television by the time they are eighteen, it is obviously important to examine the influence of the sex stereotypes to which they have been exposed in both programs and commercials. Letty Cottin Pogrebin, a writer and editor, said in a speech at Yale University in 1972:

> When the NOW group in Washington watched forty children's shows they found only four female leads and two of them were witches. . . . Check out the cartoons like "The Flintstones" and situation comedies like "I Love Lucy," and see how kids learn that women are scheming, brainless, deceptive, and frivolous: that women control their men through devious comic plots but they never possess power or dignity, that men are said to be problem solvers, workers in the world outside the home, brave and courageous when called upon. . . . Consider also occupational unreality. Over 33 million American women work, and nearly half of all married women have jobs outside the home. Yet we cannot find one female character in a children's show or situation comedy who is a wife or mother with a job outside the home. . . . Think of the millions of conflicted children whose mommies are not home perfecting a good cup of coffee or trying out a new pre-soak detergent each and every day. Are they to feel cheated and deviate because the aproned mothers in TV programs and commercials bear little resemblance to their own mothers coming home tired from a day at the factory or a crisis at the office?*

The National Organization for Women has a Media Committee which is presently involved in research in this area.

MINORITY GROUPS AND CHILDREN'S TV

Minorities on programs designed for children are as stereotyped and misrepresented as they often are on adult programs.

* *"Who Is Talking to Our Children?"* pp. 57, 58.

In a pilot study carried out for ACT by Black Efforts for Soul in Television (BEST) in Washington, D.C., children's Saturday morning programs were analyzed for racial and nonwhite emphasis. The study found that non-American and nonwhite cultures were referred to negatively almost every time they were mentioned, and that black and other minority characters made up only a small percentage of characters, with 7 percent black and 2 percent other minorities.

The analysis found that the subject of race was never mentioned or discussed, and that even in shows with black stars or characters, the blacks interacted only with white characters in a white community. Occasional black leaders had white coleaders, but most shows had white leaders. All four references to American Indians were derogatory.

RESPONSIBILITY OF THE PARENTS

Parents do indeed have the responsibility for controlling the television shows their children watch. As was pointed out earlier, there are very few programs designed specifically for children. During the hours when children normally watch television, parents must decide what adult reruns or cartoon series they will allow their children to watch. In the evening hours, when networks normally program for adults, parents have to make their own decisions about allowing their children to watch. Some parents feel that evening programs are often of higher quality than afternoon reruns and prefer to let their children watch them. Others feel that adult programs are beyond the understanding of young children, and that their viewing should be strictly limited to children's shows.

In all these cases, it is virtually impossible for anyone to define "good" and "bad" programs for children. Each parent has to make his own decision, based on knowledge of his child and individual tastes, values, and standards. Try to watch some programs with your children, talk the problem over with them if

you feel they are able to discuss it, and then make up your rules and stick to them.

QUESTIONS PARENTS ASK

Question: What's wrong with children watching cartoons?

Answer: It depends on the cartoon. If parents feel that a cartoon depicts a well-told story with animation that enhances the story, then it is probably a good program. Basically the criteria for a good program are similar no matter what the program format. "Sesame Street" uses animation in many of its segments, and so does an extremely violent Japanese-made cartoon about car-racing adventures called "Speed Racer." But the two programs are totally different. In much the same way as a story can be published as a paperback, hard-cover, a series of magazine articles, or a one-page synopsis, so a children's story idea can be translated into a variety of formats. The integrity of the interpretation, the quality of the production, and your personal taste are the only criteria that you can consistently trust.

Question: What about children watching soap operas? They're on in the afternoon when many children are home.

Answer: There are some people who find that children are bored by the talkiness of soap operas. Others are much more concerned that the child not watch real people, on the screen, suffering in an excessively dramatic fashion when he doesn't understand what's happening. Other parents feel that soap operas are like other adult programs on television and probably should not be watched by children on a regular basis. Our experience has been that the general content of most soap operas is not really designed to meet the needs of young children and that the style of presentation can often confuse and disturb them. Certainly soap operas are not considered children's programs by broadcasters, even though they are aired during daytime hours.

Question: If the programs are so bad, why don't parents just get rid of the television set?

Answer: Some parents do take that solution. On the other hand, television is so much a part of our environment today that a child will probably see it at a friend's home, at school, or in many other situations even if it is not on at home. We, as parents, have to set our children some kind of example about living with television. It is most difficult for us because our grandparents and parents didn't have to cope with this problem to such a degree. Children learn that there are rules about crossing the street, about brushing teeth, about not eating dangerous substances, and in the same way they can learn that television is one aspect of their lives which does not have to overwhelm all other activities.

Question: We are careful about what our young children see on TV, but during children's programs on commercial television there are often ads for adult movies or promotional announcements of evening shows. What can we do?

Answer: Complain loudly to the station and the network. Several times during daytime programs, one Boston station ran a promo for Hitchcock's movie *The Birds*, showing the final horrifying scenes of hundreds of birds pecking at a child. Before a recent evening children's special, another station showed a scene of a woman being strangled as the promo for a late night movie. Hundreds of children who tuned in early for the special saw one of the most violent scenes from the movie. There is no excuse for such thoughtless programing from local networks and stations. First, deal with your child's reactions and help him to feel comfortable. Then call the station and complain. Then write a letter to the station with one copy to the network with which it is affiliated and one copy to the Federal Communications Commission. (See Resource Directory for addresses.)

TELEVISION AND EDUCATION

Since children learn from everything they watch, all TV viewing is an education for them. However, teachers and others involved in education have an extra dimension in which to reach children. In schools, television is virtually controlled by the teacher and can, therefore, be examined more objectively. There are two aspects of TV and in-school education that are growing in importance:

Media in the Schools

Films and videotape, sound cassettes, and photographs are becoming part of our children's vocabulary at an earlier and earlier age. Some elementary school children have already had the experience of making their own movies and TV programs, while others may have been taken on a tour of a local television station. Teachers have found that the challenge of using the new media in the classroom is usually eminently worth the trouble of learning about them. An excellent source of information in this area is the Center for Understanding Media in New York, which provides workshops for teachers interested in learning how to use film and videotape in the classroom.

Teachers also use educational TV programs in the classroom. There is a wide range of in-school programing, on almost all subjects, provided by such groups as National Instructional Television. These groups often provide accompanying teachers' booklets and follow-up material based on a specific curriculum. (See "Television and Education" in Resource Directory.)

At the same time, teachers have found it helpful to take advantage of programs watched by children outside of school. Programs can be linked to a subject they are studying or research projects can grow out of an issue raised on a TV program. Some teachers encourage careful monitoring of programs. Students watch specific programs and look for examples of such things as sexism and racism. One teacher asks her class to watch an early evening series, and the following day encourages questions about the program—who it was designed for, why were the characters chosen, what is the story about, what is the reason for the program. In discussions like these, children can begin to analyze their viewing and to understand the necessity for critical evaluation of what they watch. In an unusual reading program involving 900 inner-city public school students in Philadelphia, children watch a videotaped program while following the written script provided for them before the class. The results show an amazing enthusiasm for reading from children who used to be bored in class and a follow-up interest in students wanting to learn typing in order to write their own scripts.

Consumer Education in the Schools

Television is the first medium to treat all children as miniature consumers and to advertise to them on their own programs. Parents and teachers, therefore, need to encourage children to cope with advertising pressures and to learn about value and prices. In-school groups can examine all aspects of advertising directed to children, and teachers can show children the different techniques of the commercials directed to them.

The Loyola University Communications Education work-texts dealing with "Persuasion" and "Mass Media" are excellent basic materials for a lively approach to this topic for older children. Teachers can help younger children to understand the concepts of advertising and why some ads might appear to be misleading. Some teachers encourage children to prepare their own commercials and examine them. One teacher in New Hampshire organized his class to file a complaint with a local television station which had advertised a simple toy that didn't work the way it promised after several children in the class bought it. Several law schools encourage students to become involved in actual communications actions and do research and file legal briefs on them.

drawing by Katrina

CHAPTER
5

"FIRST DO
NO HARM!"
VIOLENCE ON CHILDREN'S TV

In medicine a basic principle is, "First do no harm!" Television might well adopt this as its first principle for children's programing. It might meet that goal by insisting that those creative people who devise and produce programs for children become thoroughly familiar with the knowledge which already exists about child growth and development.

—Dr. Richard Granger, Yale Child Study Center*

While it is difficult to state exactly what effect watching violent programs on television will have upon individual children, it seems inconsistent with research to claim—as many broadcasters do—that it has no effect at all. Parents should watch some of the programs that their children see and make their own decisions about what to allow or ban.

The real question about violence on television is *why* it should be a part of children's programing in the first place. After all, there are a million and one other things in the world that could be the subject for children's shows. However, since there is a great deal of violence on television, much research has been con-

* *"Who Is Talking to Our Children?"* p. 8.

ducted in this area. Studies prepared for the Surgeon General's Scientific Advisory Committee on Television and Social Behavior found that children's cartoons were the most violent of all programs examined. Dr. George Gerbner of the Annenberg School of Communications, University of Pennsylvania stated:

It is . . . clear that children watching Saturday morning cartoons had the least chance of escaping violence or of avoiding the heaviest . . . saturation of violence on all television.

Dr. Gerbner found that "the average cartoon hour had nearly six times the violence rate of the average adult television drama hour."*

As an example, Dr. John Schwalter, of the Yale Child Psychiatry Unit and the Yale School of Medicine, describes what befell the

* "Violence in Television Drama: Trends and Symbolic Function," *Television and Social Behavior*, vol. 1, p. 36.

coyote in a six-minute segment of "Roadrunner," which he considers the least frightening of the cartoons for preschool children:

In minute one, a cannon blew his head off; in minute two he was pushed under a boulder; in minute three, he fell a long, long way to plop in a puff of dust to the canyon floor; in minute four, he fell again and was later blown up; in minute five, he was run over by a truck and later crushed by a rock; and in minute six he was run over yet again to total eight alleged deaths in six minutes.*

STUDIES ON VIOLENCE

Two psychology professors, Robert M. Liebert of the State University of New York and Robert A. Barton of Purdue University, told a convention of the American Psychological Association in August 1971 that their studies and increasing scientific evidence suggest that children are using violence on television as "a partial guide for their own actions."

The present entertainment of the television medium may be contributing in some measure to the aggressive behavior of many normal children. Such an effect has now been shown in a wide variety of situations.

An independent study sponsored as one of a series by the National Institute of Mental Health, showed that the behavior of preschool children changed for the worse when they were shown violent television programs and improved when they were exposed to "socially constructive" ones. The study was conducted by Dr. Aletha Stein and Dr. Lynette Friedrich, both assistant professors of human development at Pennsylvania State University, and was assisted by Dr. Fred W. Vondracek.

In this study, a group of preschool children were exposed over a four-week period to twelve programs which were classified as "aggressive" (including "Superman" and "Batman") or "prosocial" (including "Mister Rogers' Neighborhood"). The viewers of the "aggressive" programs displayed increased physical or

* *"Who Is Talking to Our Children?"* p. 11.

verbal aggression or both. Those who watched the "pro-social" programs were said to have improved their observance of rules, tolerance of delays, and perisistence at tasks. A third group, shown programs regarded as "neutral" in effect, exhibited reactions falling well between the two extremes.

In 1972, at hearings before a Senate committee, all the members of the Commission on Television and Social Behavior admitted in questioning by Senator John Pastore that there was some causal link between children who watched television violence and some aggressive behavior.

Television clearly seems to have a cumulative effect, resulting from watching not one program but a consistent pattern of programs. Parents have always known that television programs have a direct effect on children's behavior in some cases, since they have seen them act out TV-inspired situations and characters. Advertisers too are well aware that TV has a persuasive effect, and are only too willing to spend money taking advantage of it. Ironically, broadcasters consistently claim that nobody can prove specific effects of violent programing, while they never doubt the persuasive effects of the commercials shown between these programs.

In an analysis of Saturday morning children's shows on commercial television in 1971, Dr. F. Earle Barcus found that "about three out of 10 dramatic segments were 'saturated' with violence, and 71% had at least one instance of human violence with or without the use of weapons." His examination also showed that violence never seemed permanently harmful, since of the many segments with human violence, only three resulted in any visible or enduring injuries.

"This was not due to the gentle nature of the violence however," Dr. Barcus states,

since many characters were flattened by rocks, cars, or other objects, blown up by bombs and cannons, and lifted high in the sky by left hooks. They simply seem immune to violence and pop back for the next dose. . . . One is left with the impression that, after all, violence is harmless since very little permanent damage is done to the characters.*

* *Saturday Children's Television*, p. 29.

Dr. Schowalter believes that the violence and death on children's shows "probably make it harder for them to mourn actual deaths." To the argument that these are "natural" and should therefore be part of children's TV, he answers:

Unfortunately, violence and death are often portrayed in the most unnatural forms and as the most obvious, if not the only, way to settle personal problems. Invariably absent are the damage, pain, grief, mourning, destruction, and other consequences of violence in real life. . . . It is not that violence and death should never be shown on TV but that writers and producers of children's shows should take more into account what is already known about children's development.*

In a study for the Surgeon General's report *Television and Social Behavior*, Thomas F. Baldwin and Colby Lewis interviewed script writers and producers for adult programs. One writer admitted that violence in programing was an inevitable consequence of the commercial broadcasting system.

We aren't going to get rid of violence until we get rid of advertisers. The advertiser wants something with which to get the audience. Violence equals excitement equals ratings.†

There is violence on children's television because it sells products. Broadcasters and advertisers know that children will watch a fast, action-packed cartoon in preference to most other programs, which is why so many of these programs exist; action cartoons get high ratings and sell products. One mother said, "If I were telling my children a story and two men started fighting in the corner of the room, it would be very hard to stop them from watching the fight."

HOW TO REDUCE VIOLENCE ON TELEVISION

Action for Children's Television initially was formed because of concern with the excessive violence on children's television.

---

* *"Who Is Talking to Our Children?"* p. 12.
† *Television and Social Behavior*, vol. 1, p. 314.

But it soon became clear that as long as broadcasters believed that violent programs were the easiest way to get large audiences, the highest share of the ratings, and thus the most advertising dollars, they would continue to schedule violence for children.

In the long term, the only way to reduce the violence on television would be to take children's programing out of the ratings system and make it a public service area. This would mean that there would be no commercials on children's programs, but a simple one-line underwriting message could follow the shows ("This program was brought to you by the Everything Company"). In this way, advertisers would not vie for the highest possible number of viewers, but would want to be associated with a popular but high quality show which would reflect well on the company's image. Naturally, such a step would have to be implemented in the public interest by a regulatory agency such as the Federal Communications Commission.

What Can the Federal Communications Commission Do?

Theoretically, the FCC can do a great deal. The six commissioners and a chairman are appointed by the President and serve a seven-year term. They and their staff are responsible for the licensing and regulation of broadcast channels in the United States. They are committed to the concept of locally based stations serving the interests of individual communities. It is the duty of the FCC to select the best qualified local operators and to review their performance periodically to determine if they are meeting the needs of the community. The FCC grants licenses to broadcasters for three-year periods which are usually renewed almost automatically, although that was not the intention of the original mandate. The FCC has the power and the obligation to deny a license to any broadcaster who is not serving the community to the best of his ability.

The Communications Act of 1934 requires all stations to broadcast "in the public interest, convenience and necessity." The FCC has interpreted this provision as requiring fairness in the handling of controversial issues of public importance. To achieve such fairness, the FCC has promulgated a Fairness Doctrine which is the keystone of ethical broadcasting service.

The case of the Red Lion Broadcasting Company vs. the FCC in 1969 was a landmark decision in the historic assertion of the importance of broadcasting for the benefit of the public, not the convenience of the broadcaster. It stated: "It is the right of the viewers and listeners, not the right of the broadcasters, which is paramount." Much of the present activity in citizens' rights in broadcasting and in criticisms of inadequate children's programming is based on this decision.

In practical terms, however, it is the broadcaster rather than the public who has ready access to the FCC. The broadcaster usually has a lawyer in Washington, and sometimes a lobbyist as well, to make sure that his interests are represented. The headquarters of the commercial broadcasting organization, the National Association of Broadcasters, is an imposing building a few blocks from the offices of the Commission. In many ways, some subtle and some less subtle, the broadcaster can reach the commissioners and their staff. Broadcasters have adequate funds to cover their lobbying efforts, while most citizens organizations, especially those of minority groups, are made up of volunteers working on a minimal budget. Pressure to bring change is time-consuming, and few citizens groups have had the resources or the funds to compete with the affluence of the broadcasting lobby. While it should be pointed out that individual commissioners have shown outstanding commitment to the public interest, in the long run, the broadcasters' interests usually have prevailed.

FCC and Children's Television

In late 1969, the FCC announced that it wanted broadcasters to find out the needs of their communities and was compiling a primer on the "Ascertainment of Community Needs." ACT wrote to the FCC urging that a question on children's programs be part of the ascertainment, and was invited to meet with the Commission to discuss this issue. In February 1970, five ACT members met with six of the seven commissioners in a two-hour discussion, at which ACT presented the Commission with the following guidelines:

1. There shall be no sponsorship and no commercials on children's programs.
2. No performer shall be permitted to use or mention products, services or stores by brand name during children's programs, nor shall such names be included in any way during children's programs.
3. Each station shall provide daily programing for children and in no case shall this be less than fourteen hours a week, as part of its public service requirement. Provision shall be made for programing in each of the age groups specified below, and during the time periods specified below:

A. Preschool: Ages 2–5:   7 A.M.–6 P.M. daily
    7 A.M.–6 P.M. weekends
B. Primary: Ages 6–9:   4 P.M.–8 P.M. daily
    8 A.M.–8 P.M. weekends
C. Elementary: Ages 10–12: 5 P.M.–9 P.M. daily
    9 A.M.–9 P.M. weekends

A week later, the FCC released the guidelines in the form of a public notice, for comment, and a year later, January 1971, the FCC initiated an Inquiry into Children's Television.

Broadcasters, advertisers, and their lawyers filed weighty legal arguments with the FCC. ACT turned to the public and urged them to write. The response was unprecedented in the history of the FCC. Over 100,000 letters and comments were received by the FCC from individuals, groups, and organizations representing millions of people, over 98 percent of them supporting ACT's guidelines.

In 1971, the Children's Bureau was set up at the FCC with Elizabeth Roberts as its first director. Unfortunately she has left and not been replaced. It was her initiative, however, that motivated the hearings the FCC held on children's television in the fall of 1972 and January 1973. Broadcasters and advertisers were represented by their lawyers and directors. Besides Action for Children's Television, representatives from a wide range of citizens organizations also made their voices heard, including the

San Francisco Bay Area Association of Black Psychologists, the Chinese Media Committee, the National Organization for Women, the American Federation of State, County and Municipal Employees (AFL-CIO), Consumers Union, the National Association for the Education of Young Children, the National Parent-Teacher Association, HEW's Office of Child Development, and the League of United Latin American Citizens.

While the industry protested that change was impossible and that advertising never hurt anybody, the voices of the diverse citizens groups brought up the issues of minority representation, the needs of children of different ages, and the responsibility of the broadcaster to provide some programing for the child audience.

The FCC is also examining a summary of the 100,000 letters and legal documents filed on its Inquiry into Children's Television as part of the record on this issue. Possible courses of action for the Commission range from a noncommittal policy statement exhorting broadcasters to "shape up," to a rule setting down binding guidelines for children's programing as a public service area.

Much of the credit for the FCC involvement in the sensitive area of children's television should go to the chairman of the FCC, Dean Burch, who was appointed in 1970. At the first FCC meeting with ACT, he expressed his genuine concerns about children's programs, and on several occasions he devoted major speeches and public statements to the subject. His efforts to bring pressure on broadcasters to upgrade their children's programing are certainly one of the reasons for the few improvements that have occurred in recent years. In February, 1974, Dean Birch left the FCC and was replaced as chairman by one of the commissioners, Richard Wiley.

drawing by Debby

CHAPTER
6

"GIMME GIMME GIMME"

drawing by Susan

Let's assume that you have watched TV with your children. You have selected appropriate programs for them and, perhaps, limited the time that they can spend watching TV. Now what? There is one more problem relating to children's TV: the effect of commercials.

Only ad-free television avoids selling to children. On all commercial television programs for children, there is a heavy bombardment of ads for food and toys and, until recently, for vitamin

pills. In fact, there are up to twelve minutes of commercials every hour on children's Saturday morning shows (20 percent of viewing time per hour)—and sixteen minutes on other daytime programs—more than adults see in evening prime-time shows, where commercials are limited to nine and a half minutes. Children are exhorted to grow big and strong by eating one brand of bread, promised popularity in their neighborhood if they buy a certain toy, and offered excitement and adventure if they eat a special candy bar.

TELL THEM NO

Some adults who don't spend much time with young children often respond to criticism of TV ad pressures by saying, "Tell them no when they ask for things that they have seen on television, and that's enough." Of course, this is an important option for parents, but it is an oversimplification of the problem. If there was only one ad a day on children's TV, so that the parent would be badgered only once a day, the situation might not be so unbalanced. But there are many important things to which conscientious parents must say no, and ad-created demands for products increase this negative parental function. Let's remember that ads can swamp a child by exhorting him to buy a product up to twenty-four times an hour.

WHAT'S WRONG WITH SELLING TO CHILDREN?

In many ways, selling to children is unfair. Children are recognized as being less mature and educated than adults and, because of this, we try to protect them in many ways. Mrs. Joan Ganz Cooney, president of the Children's Television Workshop, which produces "Sesame Street" and "Electric Company," puts it this way:

If we as a total society put the interest of our children first, then we are led to the inescapable conclusion that it is terribly wrong to be pitching products at the young. It is like shooting fish in a barrel. It is grotesquely unfair.*

For some reason, while we don't allow teachers to sell products to children in schools, we accept selling to children on television. If a salesman rang our doorbell and said, "Hi, I'm your friendly neighborhood toy salesman and I'd like to come into your living room and show your four-year-old a few toys while you go on cooking in the kitchen. I'll just show him the toys and he can tell you what he likes," as responsible adults we'd slam the door in his face. We know that most four-year-olds couldn't cope with a fast-talking toy salesman. Yet this happens every day on commercial television. We allow salesmen into our living rooms

* *"Who Is Talking to Our Children?"* p. 45.

through television and not only do we allow them on adult programs, but we allow them on programs specifically designed for children which reach very young audiences.

How Children Reason

In a speech given to the Advertising Club of Boston in November 1971, Dr. Freda Rebelsky, Professor of Psychology and Director of the Doctoral Program in Developmental Psychology at Boston University, summarized what we have learned about children's perceptions.

"Children are creatures that look somewhat like us, and we see them essentially as little adults," she said. But "all recent research suggests that the sense we have that children are only quantitatively different from adults is just plain wrong."

"The child is an active organizer of the world. He does not see and think about what we present, but what he can understand and use in what we present." She outlined the ways in which the organizing principles of young children (aged one to eight) differ from that of adults:

1. Children use language differently from adults. Though they may use the same words as adults do, their feelings and understandings about words are different.

   Children are, thus, apt to misinterpret information in advertisements.

2. Children use language less flexibly than adults. After they have described something one way it is difficult for them to describe it some other way.

   This would account for their tendency to interpret advertising literally. One mother, for example, found her young son cleaning the table with toothpaste. Asked why, he explained: "It worked for me, so it should work for the table."

3. Children cannot think in an orderly, logical fashion since they cannot rehearse in their heads or try different solutions or free themselves from their personal interpretations of things. They cannot as easily separate fantasy and reality.

   For this reason, a child would be unable to analyze and judge an ad or to discount its extravagant claims.

4. Even real objects in the world are not constant. A doll without an arm is not the same as a doll with an arm. A sandwich cut on the diagonal is not the same sandwich if it is cut into rectangles.
5. Children look to adults to find out what is "good" and "bad." Experimenters with children report over and over that children are concerned with what adults do and say, even strange adults whom they will never see again.

    Most commercials are delivered by adults, and children are especially susceptible to favorite host characters, whom they trust.

Dr. Rebelsky stated "with certainty" that children's feelings and ideas about TV and commercials are different from those of adults.

Dr. Richard I. Feinbloom, Medical Director of the Family Health Care Program of Harvard Medical School, wrote a letter, submitted by ACT to the FTC for its hearing on the "Impact of Advertising on Consumers" in November 1971, expressing his concern that all advertising directed to young children is "misleading" because children normally distort reality in accordance with their own immature view of the world:

> To children, normally impulsive, advertisements for appealing things demand immediate gratification. An advertisement to a child has the quality of an order, not a suggestion. The child lacks the ability to set priorities, to determine relative importance, and to reject some directives as inappropriate. It is no wonder that children are unable to make a mental correction for the distortion of a piece of merchandise as presented on television, particularly when it is dramatically portrayed with booming voices of announcers, excited child participants and rousing musical background.

Aaron Locker of Averman, Green & Locker, general counsel to the Toy Manufacturers of America, gave the advertisers' point of view in his statement to the FTC on behalf of the TMA:

> Children's attitudes toward commercials are different from the established beliefs of adults. They are more open-minded, more attracted to them. In fact small children have as much interest and warmth for the commercial as for the show.

It seems incredible that anyone should even consider advertising to a three-year-old, knowing how little he understands of what is going on in the world. But it is done all the time on programs that advertisers know are designed for three-year-olds.

MISLEADING INFORMATION IN ADS

Many people are concerned about the misinformation contained in the ads that children see. For example, many foods advertised to children—snacks, candies, cookies, oversugared cereals—lead to poor nutrition habits. Nutritionists and doctors are particularly concerned about food ads since they know that eating habits formed in childhood are extremely difficult to change. Brand-name ads are almost the only food information children receive on TV; they rarely hear of the value of eating vegetables, fresh fruits, cheese, eggs, milk, and orange juice. Instead, glamorized ads for sugar-coated foods, which lead to an excessive craving for sugar, predominate. Ads for toys or other child-oriented products often misrepresent the product by putting it in an unrealistic situation, i.e., in a group of happy friends, a luxurious and idyllic home situation, or a beautiful outdoor setting.

In March 1973, in testimony before the Senate Select Committee on Nutrition and Human Needs in Washington, D.C., Action for Children's Television stated:

A medium which could be a powerful educational tool to inform the American public of good health and nutrition is instead a vehicle for falsehood, misinformation and misleading persuasion. TV advertising presents several dangers to the health of children—the most significant are dental caries, the exclusion of more nutritious foods from the diet, obesity, and other health problems which arise in adulthood as a result of a taste for sweets acquired during childhood.

The consumption of non-nutritious and sugared foods as snacks is a major cause of dental caries. In a study of several hundred five-year-olds, a direct correlation was found between the number of snacks they ate and the number of caries in their teeth. Those who ate one snack had a caries score of 4.8; two snacks, 5.7; three snacks, 8.5; and four or more snacks, 9.8.

This is because what matters is not the *amount* of sugar ingested but the frequency of intake.* An analysis of ads directed to children on a recent Saturday morning found that almost all of the food products were for sweet, sticky snack foods, the most likely to cause caries.

Dr. Jean Mayer, Professor of Nutrition at the Harvard School of Public Health, has stated:

> Unfortunately, those cereals most heavily advertised to children are sugar-coated cereals (a number of which contain over fifty percent sugar and therefore ought not to be properly called cereals). . . . The promotion of high sugar cereals, snacks and soft drinks to children is a dental disaster.†

The Federal Trade Commission is empowered to stop any specific abuses of misleading ads and is examining the whole area of advertising to children. But there is still no independent agency of any kind that reviews ads aired during daytime hours when many children are watching television, nor are there any independent guidelines which can be enforced relating to TV advertising to children.

PREMIUMS

A growing trend in advertising to children is to push products for which children would have no use by using premium offers as a bait. Recently a commercial during a children's program showed a selection of small Noah's Ark figures which children could get "free" if they bought eight gallons of a certain brand of gasoline. Ads for frozen dinners promise children that they can find puzzles and games on the package. Several restaurants now promote child-oriented images to entice children to bring their parents there to eat.

---

* Dr. Abraham Nizel, *Nutrition in Preventive Dentistry: Science and Practice* (Philadelphia: W. B. Saunders Co., 1972), p. 35.
† March 5, 1973, at Senate Select Committee on Nutrition and Human Needs.

In cold fact, the child is being used as a salesman by the television advertisers who want to reach the adult consumer of gasoline, frozen dinners, or meals at restaurants. While the parent can certainly say no to such practices, it seems unfair for American business to use children to sell its products in this way.

VITAMIN PILL ADS

Until the summer of 1972, there were ads urging children to buy vitamin pills which were "just like candy." Many of these pills were fortified with iron, which is toxic in large quantities, and bottles of the pills were marked "keep out of the reach of children." Several leading pediatricians have vehemently criticized the idea of selling any pills "like candy" to children.

ACT taped several of the television ads for children's vitamin pills, transcribed them, and estimated the number of these being shown on children's TV shows. This basic information was followed up with research in poison centers in a few large cities, including examining statistics of the National Poison Center. It was found that vitamin overdose accounts for the second highest number of poisonings in children under five years of age throughout the United States (aspirin is the first). In one case a four-year-old boy in Kansas City, Missouri, ate a whole bottle of iron-fortified vitamin pills "to make me grow big and strong." He spent two days in intensive care in a hospital, recovering from that overdose.

The research was put together into a petition to the Federal Trade Commission, urging the elimination of vitamin pill advertising directed to children. ACT representatives presented this petition to the FTC during testimony at FTC hearings on advertising in November 1971. This move was followed up with complaints to the FTC about specific vitamin pill ads.

The petition and the complaints received extensive coverage

in the press and radio and TV news. During the spring of 1972 ACT monitors found that the number of vitamin pill ads on TV was going down, and in June 1972, the three major advertisers of children's vitamin pills voluntarily withdrew all their ads from children's TV shows. In a letter to ACT, one of the manufacturers stated:

We have become increasingly convinced that continued advertising of our children's vitamin supplement products in the present type of environment of children's programs has become no longer in our interest; this relates especially to some of the highly questionable programing as well as the number and nature of commercials presently being aired in the Saturday morning time period.

To date, the Federal Trade Commission has not acted to set any definite regulations in this area. But it is essential that some protective ruling be established. In January 1974, some vitamin pill ads directed to children were reappearing on afternoon cartoon shows.

HOST SELLING

In response to pressures from organizations like ACT and other concerned citizens, the voluntary code of the National Association of Broadcasters ruled on one aspect of advertising to children. As of 1972 the rules now state:

Children's program hosts or primary cartoon characters shall not be utilized to deliver commercial messages within or adjacent to the programs which feature such hosts or cartoon characters. This provision shall also apply to lead-ins to commercials when such lead-ins contain sell copy or imply endorsement of the product by program host or primary cartoon characters.*

* The Television Code, National Association of Broadcasters, 17th ed., April 1973, New York, p. 11.

The ruling, however, does not go so far as to prohibit host characters from selling during other children's programs *not* adjacent to programs in which they appear. Some critics also admit confusion about the definition of a primary cartoon character. But this is a constructive first step toward eliminating host selling and endorsements to children.

CHAPTER
7
HOW TO WIN THE SELLING GAME

There are different ways of helping children to cope with the pressures of attractive but misleading ads. In an article in *Woman's Day* in November 1972 entitled "Teaching a Child to Think," Fredelle Maynard stated:

Critical thinking is not just the habit of criticizing; it involves the ability to suspend judgment, to examine before accepting, to consider alternatives before making a choice. In developing this art, children need all the help they can get—and they should get it early.

Reasoning and discussion can stimulate an older child to learn how to judge advertising and to make his own decisions. But it is unreasonable to expect a preschool child, who is having trouble tying his shoelace, to demonstrate the same capabilities. One conscientious mother watching TV with her five-year-old, carefully explained that the Jumbo Truck being advertised would not really look the same in the store, that it didn't come with all the extra parts being shown, and that it would probably break very easily. The child nodded wisely and even repeated back some of her phrases. Then, turning back to the screen, the child said firmly, "I want a Jumbo Truck for my birthday."

Preschool children are just too young to comprehend the intricacies of commercialism on their own programs and too inexperienced to make reasoned consumer judgements, no matter how much information they are given.

Parents can:

• • • Watch commercials with children and try to put the exaggerated claims into perspective. "You know that film is speeded up and no car can really go that fast." Or, "Isn't that the toy in the cereal that broke the last time we got it?"

• • • Teach children to write their own commercials and reason out why certain kinds of statements are made.

• • • Analyze the specific appeal of the commercial. "I bet everyone thinks they'll get all those friends if they buy that game, but of course they don't." Or, "How can any food make you grow big so fast—that's ridiculous."

• • • Take children to the store and compare the ad with the actual product, if you think this will be effective. Some parents feel that this is too tempting and that they will end up buying the product because of pleading from the child, even if they feel it has been misrepresented.

• • • Only watch noncommercial children's television so that young children won't be exposed to commercials.

• • • Ask your doctor or school nurse for a simple poster or chart of nutritional needs for growing children, or design one yourself if you feel creative. In order to counteract food advertisements on television, educate your children about the kinds of foods they need to eat for healthy growth.

• • • Make rules about breakfast cereals—the most common product advertised to children. Some parents refuse to buy any cereal with a premium in the box. Other parents refuse to buy a cereal in which sugar is the first—which means that it is the major—ingredient listed. Other parents, having found that many of the "junk" cereals are bought for premiums or free offers and never get eaten, will only buy a cereal again if it is eaten up the first time.

• • • Encourage children to eat healthy snacks instead of prepackaged cakes and cookies, and have them easily available for children to find.

ACT has published a Nutrition Survival Kit designed to help parents educate their children to avoid highly sugared TV-advertised snacks and cereals. The kit, available from ACT, suggests alternative snacks including carrots, tomatoes, biscuits, crackers, cheese, fruits, popcorn, pretzels, peanut butter, and nuts.

QUESTIONS PARENTS ASK

Question: When I was a kid there were ads on radio, and they didn't hurt me. Sure, I wrote off for things and found out if they worked or not. Isn't being exposed to ads part of a child's education?

Answer: Yes—and no. Radio never, never had the same amount of advertising directed to children that a child experiences on television today. Even television has never before had so many commercials. In fact, when television began, children's TV shows were aired without commercials as a matter of course. But since the 1960s, the advertising scene has changed so that children are treated as a consumer market, just as adults are.

Consumer-education-by-experience is certainly one way to learn, but it is doubtful whether any three-year-old who ordered a product advertised on a preschool program that didn't perform the way he thought it would would have the mental ability to understand what had really happened. Dr. John Condry, Assistant Professor of Human Development and Psychology at Cornell University, believes that young children blame themselves when products don't perform as depicted on television, since they are unable to understand that the advertiser was trying to put his product in the best light. Children don't comprehend the complexities behind television commercials.

Broadcasters who care about informing and educating children about consumer education could produce informative messages for children's programs and save their product ads for adults. But as Cleo Hovel, of the Leo Burnett Ad Agency, said, "Our primary goal is to sell products to children, not educate them."*

Question: Don't you think worry about advertising to children is exaggerated? Surely most advertisers don't really mean to take advantage of young children!

Answer: Sadly, many do. In countless meetings with advertisers and in reading trade magazines such as *Advertising Age* and *Television and Radio Age,* we have learned that advertisers consider children only as "a market" and plan campaigns to reach the "2 to 11 year old market." One advertising executive said in *Advertising Age* (July 19, 1965):

When you sell a woman on a product and she goes into the store and finds your brand isn't in stock, she'll probably forget about it.

* *Advertising Age,* July 19, 1965.

But when you sell a kid on your product, if he can't get it, he will throw himself on the floor, stamp his feet and cry. You can't get a reaction like that out of an adult.

Eugene S. Mahany of Needham, Harper and Steers Advertising Agency wrote in *Broadcasting* magazine (June 30, 1969):

> We can shape our future marketing programs on what appeals directly to the child, not to the parent, because if the parent initiates interest, then the appeal is lessened, and the job of selling is made more difficult.

Certainly there are some responsible advertisers for child-oriented products. Fisher-Price, for example, advertises its line of preschool toys only to parents. But most manufacturers will listen to any advertising suggestion that will sell products, even if that means selling to children.

TOYS: THE ATAC CHRISTMAS SURVIVAL KIT

A few years ago, ACT created its first subdivision, ATAC (Advice on Toys at Christmas). It published a simple leaflet to help parents cope with the pressures of toy selling around the holidays, which is reprinted below. Perhaps it can help you too.

Background for Survival

> "Mommy, please buy me that toy . . ."
> "I want that and that and that . . ."
> "Buy me that toy—it's on T.V."
> "Look at that commercial—that's what I want."

Around Christmas the television barrages us with ads that glamorize toys and tantalize our children. Our youngsters become miniature salesmen, nagging us to buy specific toys. But when we do, we often find them overpriced and inferior in quality. This results partly from the very pressures of the advertising.

A toy dealer in Berkeley, California, wrote to ACT describing "a sponge rubber ball that would sell 'plain' for 29–39 cents, packaged and televised the retail price is—$1.29!" He also told us that television toy commercials have created "giant toy manufacturers who stifle competition and force stores to take unwanted merchandise."

And *Playthings*, the trade magazine for the toy industry, stated in its 1969 annual survey of the toy and hobby trade:

> . . . repeatedly, both retailers and wholesalers returned surveys with harsh words for the TV-advertised toys; these items were most often labeled as over-priced and below standard—a contributing problem to after Christmas clean-up because "TV toys come back in droves . . . they just don't work properly."

Both TV and toy manufacturers make a lot of money from us and our children around Christmas. Did you know that ads on TV cost more in the months before Christmas? For example, sixty seconds of commercial time Saturday morning on CBS cost $8,300 on April 12, 1970, while on November 15 the cost jumped to $11,500. NBC charged $6,100 in April and $7,400 in November—and ABC put its price up from $5,300 to $8,500.

Did you know that networks always run many *more* commercials during children's Saturday morning shows than you ever see in evening prime-time shows?

Did you know that many stations put on children's shows (usually old cartoons) *only* before Christmas in order to take advantage of the toy advertising?

Did you know that many advertising agencies have highly skilled research departments to analyze exactly how to play on a child's desires? They test and retest ads to make sure that they really hit home. As columnist Bob Mackenzie of the *Oakland Tribune* put it in an article on March 31, 1970:

> The rocking, socking hard sell of the children's ads makes adult commercials sound like apologetic murmurs. The products they hawk are universally vile, from gooey confectionery to fantastically expensive mechanical toys with aggressive personalities and feeble machinery. The makers of $15 toys know that Junior must be worked up to fever pitch if he is to have sufficient fanatical gleam in his eye to wrest that much cash from Dad. So they pour on the juice.

And did you know that many experts believe that children do not need the complex mechanical kinds of toys advertised on television? Dr. James L. Hymes, Jr., Professor of Education and Chairman of the Early Childhood Education Department of the University of Maryland writes in his book *The Child Under Six*:

The essence of children's play is that the youngsters build their own meanings and ideas into whatever is at hand. The children themselves are the "toy manufacturers." You don't really have to spend much cash for finished products which have the details worked out.*

Indeed, one toy executive admitted that when boxes of new toys are tested on a group of children, the children end up playing games with the empty boxes and ignoring the complicated toys! Television toy ads do not encourage the use of imaginative play and, indeed, television toys may be detrimental to the creative use of simple playthings.

So don't feel guilty about saying no to a TV toy that you don't think is going to be a good present. You have right on your side from the highest places!

Survival Action 1:
What You Should Look for in Toys

1. Is the toy worth the price? Will it hold your child's attention beyond Christmas Day? An expensive toy should be made to last and provide long-term enjoyment.
2. Does your child expect too much from the toy? Often children are bitterly disappointed when they actually see the TV toy they wanted so desperately. Sit down with them on Saturday morning and see how the toys are advertised. Compare this with the products in the stores.
3. Is your child the right age for the toy? TV ads rarely mention an age range—after all, Saturday morning programs are geared to a "2 to 11-year-old" audience, network executives tell us.
4. Does the toy have batteries or complicated mechanical parts? Remember—these are the first things to go wrong.
5. Is the toy safe? Sadly, only you can judge whether or not a toy is safe. There is a Child Protection and Toy Safety Act on the books,

* Englewood Cliffs, N.J.: Prentice-Hall, 1961, p. 193.

but it is poorly enforced. Be wary of toys that require electricity (one toy stove reached temperatures of over 300 degrees), shoot objects in the air, or have sharp edges or unfinished surfaces which could hurt your child. Small children try to put things in their mouths, so be wary of loose parts. Think of how a child might misuse the toy.

The newly created Consumer Product Safety Commission has begun to check on unsafe banned toys in the stores, using consumers to do the investigating, and promises to serve as an active watchdog in the area of product safety. The Food and Drug Administration also lists dangerous toys on occasion and a "List of Banned Products" is available from the Consumer Information Center.

Survival Action 2:
What You Can Do to Influence the Industry

1. Complain! Write to a manufacturer if you don't like his product. Write even if you did *not* buy his product, and tell him why. His name and address will be on the box. Remember that toy manufacturers are in business to please you. Tell them what you want—they do care.

2. Buy carefully. Your purchases speak clearly to the manufacturer. If you buy, he assumes that he's made what you want. Look for a store with a wide selection of toys, and choose the one you can afford. If you object to advertising directed to children, don't buy TV toys.

3. Tell grandparents, relatives, and friends about ATAC. It might help them to survive the selling pressures too.

A LONG-TERM SOLUTION

If it were possible to take commercialism out of children's programing, as is done at present on public television, the key question is: Who would pay for the programing?

Since broadcasters make great profits on most of their programing, ACT has always believed that children's television is one area in which they should consider the public service factor above the profit motive. Dr. William Melody, an associate professor of communications economics at the Annenberg School of Communications at the University of Pennsylvania, carried out an extensive study into the economic characteristics of advertising practices directed to children and how they affect programing. Tracing the history of children's television, he showed how in the early years quality children's shows were used as an incentive to promote the sale of television sets while today poor quality, commercial-laden programs exploit the economic potential of child consumers. He also offered solutions for alternate financing of children's television, based on the gradual phasing out of advertising directed to children over a period of years, without causing significant financial hardship to the broadcast industry. He recommended alternative funding from a variety of sources such as foundations, institutional advertising by corporations, and underwriting by major companies and institutions.

He also pointed out the unique "repeatability" of children's programs. After a few years there is always a whole new generation of children who are as happy to watch the same programs as were the previous children. Children's programs can be "banked" and repeated almost indefinitely, so that it is worthwhile making the initial investment of programing of the highest possible quality.*

For the interim between the present situation and the slow phasing out of advertising ACT has long suggested several ways for improving children's TV programing: clustering commercials at a couple of specific times each hour, rather than interrupting the body of the program; allowing *fewer commercials*; eliminating commercials for products harmful to children's health.

In the summer of 1973, the newly appointed chairman of the Federal Trade Commission, Lewis Engman, made a major speech in which he said:

* William Melody, *Children's Television: The Economics of Exploitation.*

If television advertising deceives children, if it frustrates them through false or misleading promises, if it promotes the sale of dangerous toys or other products, if it fosters dietary habits which endanger their health—if it does these things, I think television advertising which is directed at children will soon find itself circumscribed by legal restrictions and requirements.*

Following this speech, a committee representing industry and consumer groups was set up to try to devise an acceptable code for children's TV advertising. Certain basic disagreements soon made themselves felt in early meetings and the consumer representatives realized that the industry was not going to compromise. Consequently, representatives from Action for Children's Television, Consumers Federation of America, Consumers Union, the Council on Children, Merchandising, and Media, and from two California legal groups met separately and designed a Code for Children's TV Advertising acceptable to them. This was presented to the Federal Trade Commission and to the industry in January 1974, for consideration and possible implementation.

According to the Code:

1. No children's commercial† shall:

   a. Offer a premium or membership conditioned on a purchase.

   b. Use a children's program lead personality or host, any sports or entertainment personality, any figure in the news or any primary cartoon character.

   c. Include any testimonial by fictional or real life characters.

   d. Advertise any product or service introduced after July 1, 1974, which uses in its name a children's program lead personality or host, any sports or entertainment personality, any figure in the news, any primary cartoon character or any program name.

   e. Use children as spokespersons or employ them to deliver sales messages.

   f. Use disclaimer titles without a simultaneous audio disclosure.

---

* Speech to the American Bar Association, August 1973.
† Commercial on a program for which children (aged two through eleven) are more than 50 percent of the audience.

g. Advertise any vitamin preparation or over-the-counter drug.

h. Advertise any product which is dangerous to children or carries on its label a warning discouraging use by children.

i. Advertise any edible product or beverage containing sugar over 15 percent by wet weight or 35 percent by dry weight.

j. Identify or imply fruit or other characterizing ingredient or flavor without disclosing its natural/artificial nature as proposed . . . under the Food, Drug and Cosmetic Act.

k. Claim directly or by implication that any edible product or nutrient of itself produces, hastens, or enhances vigor, stamina, strength, energy, growth, or intellectual performance. Caloric value may be stated.

l. Advertise any motion picture which is not rated "G."

m. Reinforce racial or sexual stereotyping.

2. No family commercial* shall:

a. Advertise any product which is dangerous to children or carries on its label a warning discouraging use by children.

b. Advertise any edible product or beverage containing sugar over 15 percent by wet weight or 35 percent by dry weight, without an audio and video warning that eating the product between meals may be harmful to a child's teeth.

3. No clock hour containing a children's program shall include:

a. More than six minutes of non-program material.

b. More than two minutes of commercials for games and toys, or for edible products, or for any other single category of products or services.

c. More than one commercial for any single product or product line (including its accessories) or for any single service.

d. More than two commercial breaks approximately at the hour and half-hour which shall be preceded by an announcement that commercials follow.

4. No clock hour containing a family program shall include more than 9½ minutes of non-program material.

* Commercial on a program for which children are more than 20 but less than 50 percent of the audience.

5. No promotional announcement in or near a children's program shall promote an adult program.

The adoption of this code could be the first step in a long-term plan to phase out all advertising in or near television programs for children, which would benefit our children and improve the programing designed for them.

drawing by Rob Chalfen

CHAPTER
8

CHILDREN'S
WORKBOOK

How much TV do you watch? What do you do the rest of the time? Which programs do you like? The next few pages have several charts for you to complete which will help you to answer those questions.

DIARY AND KEY TO ACTIVITIES

This is to be completed for one full week—or several days. Keep it handy and check how many squares are filled in with TV watching compared to your other activities.

TV TESTING CHART

This chart is for you to make notes on what programs you watch and why. Keep it near the television set with a pencil and check it off as you watch.

PROGRAM RATING CHART

Now you can be a critic. Choose some specific programs you watch, and write down your criticisms and ratings for them. You can do this with any program and grade it in any way you want.

DIARY

	MON.	TUES.	WED.
7–8 A.M.			
8–9 A.M.			
9–10 A.M.			
10–11 A.M.			
11–12 A.M.			
12–1 P.M.			
1–2 P.M.			
2–3 P.M.			
3–4 P.M.			
4–5 P.M.			
5–6 P.M.			
6–7 P.M.			
7–8 P.M.			

SUGGESTED KEY

 Watched TV   Read   Played outside

obc School   Slept   Went to friends

DIARY

THURS.	FRI.	SAT.	SUN.

¶O¶ Ate

$2 \times / \cdot 2$ Did homework

Went out with parents

Played with brother/sister

Played alone inside

Design other symbols for your other activities.

YOUR TV TESTING CHART

	MON.	TUES.	WED.
Date			
Program Title and Time on			
Who chose and Why			
Program Title and Time on			
Who chose and Why			
Program Title and Time on			
Who Chose and Why			
Program Title and Time on			
Who Chose and Why			

Put this near your TV set and fill it in.

YOUR TV TESTING CHART

THURS.	FRI.	SAT.	SUN.

PROGRAM RATING CHART

Name of program and station or network it is on	Length of program and number of commercials	Description of program

PROGRAM RATING CHART

8 7 od	6 5 4 OK	3 2 1 Poor	Comments

EXPERIMENTS FOR YOUR TV VIEWING

Experiment 1: The Turn-Off

Try setting aside a definite period of time for not watching TV at all. It might be a few days, a full week, a weekend. But make it a defi-

1. EXPERIMENT: THE TURN-OFF

	MON.	TUES.	WED.
7–8 A.M.			
8–9 A.M.			
9–10 A.M.			
10–11 A.M.			
11–12 A.M.			
12–1 P.M.			
1–2 P.M.			
2–3 P.M.			
3–4 P.M.			
4–5 P.M.			
5–6 P.M.			
6–7 P.M.			
7–8 P.M.			

What did you do when you turned off TV? (You can use the Key to Activities from the Diary)

nite time, and keep a careful diary of what you do instead of watching TV. You can then compare that with your chart for viewing times. Maybe you could ask your parents or grandparents what they did when they didn't have television.

THE TURN-OFF

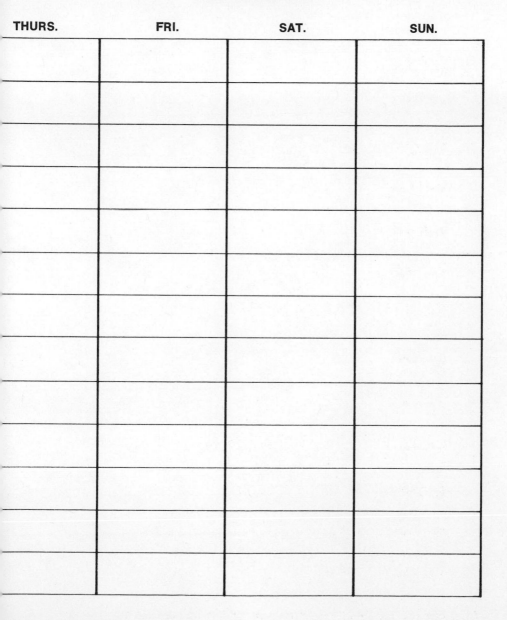

THURS.	FRI.	SAT.	SUN.

Experiment 2: My Perfect Viewing Room

Imagine you could design your own Video Space which would be the ideal place for watching television. What would it look like? What would it need? Where should it be? Why would it be perfect? Write a description of your perfect viewing room or draw it.

Experiment 3: Design Your Own Program

You've probably seen dozens of television programs. What do you remember about them? What did you like or dislike? How were they put together?

Imagine that someone gave you half an hour of TV time to produce your own program. What would you put into those minutes—news, discussion, puppets, movies, sports? Plan it out—it's all yours. (Begin here and then use as many sheets of paper as you need.)

TV Show title: . . . .   Length: . . . .

Producer: . . . .   Staff: . . . .

Opening shot: . . . .

(For a TV script you write the action in one column and the dialogue in another:

Shot of cowboy on horse.	JEFF: Where did you last see the wild stallion?
Pan to horizon and clouds.	MIKE: Out there to the west.)

CONSUMERISM

An eleven-year-old girl named Dawn Ann Kurth from Melbourne, Florida, became interested in advertising to children because of her younger sister:

"My sister Martha, who is 7, had asked my mother to buy a box of Post Raisin Bran so that she could get the free record that was on the back of the box. It had been advertised several times on Saturday morning cartoon shows. My mother bought the cereal, and we all (there are four children in our family) helped Martha eat it so she could get the record.

"It was after the cereal was eaten and she had the record that the crisis occurred. There was no way the record would work.

"Martha was very upset and began crying and I was angry too. It just didn't seem right to me that something could be shown on TV that worked fine and people were listening and dancing to the record and when you bought the cereal, instead of laughing and dancing, we were crying and angry."

Dawn had been chosen with thirty-five other students at Meadow-lane Elementary School to do a project in any field they wanted. She decided to find out how other children felt about deceptive advertising. She began by watching television one Saturday morning, and clocked twenty-five commercial messages during one hour, 8:00 to 9:00, not counting ads for shows coming up or public service announcements. She also discovered that during shows her parents liked to watch there were only ten to twelve commercials each hour, which surprised her.

Dawn devised a questionnaire and asked 1,538 children the following questions:

Quiz

1. Do you ask your mother to buy products you see advertised on TV? Yes   No
2. Did you ever buy a product to get the free bonus gift inside? Yes   No
3. Were you satisfied? Yes   No
4. Write down an example.
5. Do you believe that certain products you see advertised on TV make you happier or have more friends? Yes   No
6. Please write an example.
7. Did you ever feel out of it because your mother wouldn't buy a certain product? Yes   ˙No
8. Did you ever feel your mother was mean because she wouldn't buy the product you wanted? Yes   No

Answer these questions yourself.*

---

* Dawn got the following responses to her questionnaire: 1) Yes, 1,203; No 330. 2) Yes 1,120; No 413. 3) Yes 668; No 873. 5) Yes 1,113; No 420. 7) Yes 802; No 735. 8) Yes 918;

Some adults concerned with advertising to children heard about Dawn's study, and Senator Frank E. Moss invited her to appear before the Senate Subcommittee for Consumers at special hearings on May 31, 1972. Dawn's testimony explained her concerns and outlined the survey she had carried out. Her testimony is now part of the Senate record of the hearings.

For You to Do: Do Your Own Think!

What do you think about advertising to children?

Can you think of ways to help young children understand about ads on television?

Does anything bother you about some of the ads you may see?

What do you like about ads on television?

If there had to be ads on television, how many would be the ideal number for you in one hour?

Write down your answers on a sheet of paper.

DO-IT-YOURSELF

Your Own Cartoon

You must have seen plenty of TV cartoons. Did you know that each cartoon is made up of hundreds and hundreds of drawings, which are then filmed?

On the next two pages are a series of squares for you to design your own cartoon story. It can be anything at all. It can look like anything at all. It's all yours! (You can turn the book sideways if you want.)

THIS CARTOON IS CALLED:

Your Own Public Service Announcement (PSA)

When advertisers make a commercial or public service announcement they prepare a story board, with drawings of how they think the finished commercial will look. Later it is possible to show what the PSA

"THE AWARD"

Courtesy of Leo Burnett Company, Inc., and the National Dairy Council.

1. (Silent pullup)

2. (Music under) BULL: We're here to present the award for the best group. Nominees are...

3. ...Vegetables and Fruits...

4. ...Green Leafy and Citrus Productions.

5. COW: Milk Group...

6. ...Cow Productions.

looked like on television by using photos from the film with the words underneath.

Look at this example, and then fill out the blank story board on pp. 110–11 with your own public service announcement. (You can turn the book sideways if you want.)

7. BULL: Meat Group...

8. ...Meat, Fish, Chicken, Eggs and Cheese Productions.

9. COW: Breads and Cereals...

10. ...Whole Grain and Enriched Cereals Productions.

11. BULL: The envelope, please.

12. Why, they all win.

13. COW: Kids, you'll win with the four basic food groups every day.

14. BULL: Parents, you'll win, too.

15. (Music up and out)

THIS PSA IS FOR:

Bubble Gum Fights Back!

Topps Chewing Gum recently included some crazy commercial cards in some of these packets of bubble gum.* Here are a few to show you a new way of thinking about commercials.

* "Wacky Packages" is the registered trademark of Topps Chewing Gum, Inc.

CHAPTER
9

YOU CAN MAKE
A DIFFERENCE

Perhaps you have read this far and feel that broader action needs to be taken in the sensitive area of children's television programing. Perhaps you are personally involved with children through education or medicine or as a parent. You've come to your own family decisions about how much television to watch and, as best you can, are helping your own children to cope with the pressures of programing and ads. You feel that since you are meeting your responsibility, you would like to put some pressure on the broadcaster to meet his responsibility to put on more and better programs. Children's television will always be a joint responsibility—shared between the parents, with their natural concern for their own children, and the broadcaster, with his sometimes less apparent concern for the needs of the children in the community he is serving.

ALWAYS WRITE

One of the most effective ways to make your voice heard in these days of instant communication is the good, old-fashioned letter. If you see something on television that you like very much, or that bothers you for some reason or other, or that you feel is unsuitable for children, compose a sensible and thoughtful letter clearly stating your feelings. Type it if you possibly can; handwritten letters don't get the same kind of attention in executive offices as typed letters do. Make some carbon copies and send them out, too—as many as you like. And type the names of the people you're sending them to at the bottom of your letter.

For example, you could write a letter to a *local station*, expressing your feelings about the cartoons they are running. In that case, send a copy to the Federal Communications Commission in Washington, D.C. (which keeps a file on every licensed station), and to the network with which the station is affiliated. When the FCC receives a "Complaint," it usually asks the station to respond, and, very rarely, investigates it. The FCC has the power, however, to levy a fine or issue an order demanding the station to remedy the complaint. In a Complaint, state your name, the station call letters, and your specific complaint or suggestion.

If possible, relate this to an FCC Standard (*see* Appendix). Ask for a specific remedy.

You might write a letter to the *sponsor*. Let the sponsor or advertisers know how you feel about programs on which their product ads appear, or about advertising directed to children, or about the performance of the product. You should send a copy of letters like this to the station that aired the ad (or the network), the FCC, and the Federal Trade Commission in Washington, D.C.

You might write directly to the *network* that originated the program, and send a copy to the local station that aired it and to the FCC and the sponsor.

You might write letters to the *Federal Communications Commission*. The FCC licenses every TV and radio station for three years and is responsible for ensuring that stations meet "the public interest, convenience and necessity." Part of the station's responsibility is to meet the needs of the large child audience which most of them are reaching. The 100,000 letters, filings and comments that the FCC received in its recent inquiry on children's television were a persuasive factor in encouraging it to continue the examination of this area.

You might cite specific abuses in advertising to the *Federal Trade Commission*. The FTC is responsible for eliminating unfair or misleading advertising and can accept complaints relating to specific ads.

You could write to the *Food and Drug Administration* in Rockville, Maryland, about food advertising or about specific edible products that are advertised to children on TV. The FDA is also concerned with the sale of dangerous toys.

As a citizen, you can write to *your congressman* and let him or her know your concerns about children's television and advertising. It is always helpful to inform your congressman about issues such as this so that he will know where his constituency stands on such matters.

And try sending letters to *the press*. Your local TV critic is probably well aware of what is going on in children's TV and would be glad to hear from you. The editor of a weekly paper might be glad to discuss this issue with a local resident and to air it in the pages of his paper.

And Don't Forget the Praise!

It is often easy to type off a letter of indignation when the movie about the Boston Strangler is aired at 7:00 P.M. and scares the wits out of your children who watch some of it before you can turn it off. But don't forget to write the letter complimenting a station that airs a good children's program at a reasonable hour or a station that is making efforts to cluster commercials at the beginnings and ends of children's programs. And send copies of the letters of praise as well as the letters of complaint. That's only fair! Most station managers are sensitive to letters from the public.

Never Underestimate the Power of a Letter

If it is a good clear letter, based on clearly stated facts, chances are that the message will get through to the right place. Don't be afraid to call up and follow through on it if you don't get a reply; that will make doubly sure that it doesn't get ignored.

Useful Addresses

In the Resource Directory is a list of useful addresses of people to whom you may want to write. You can look up the addresses of your local TV stations in the phone book under their call letters (WNAC TV, KTVU TV, etc.) if you need to write to them.

BE INFORMED

It is important, when dealing with any controversial issue, to make sure that you have done your homework and know as much as you possibly can about your subject. This is essential in an area as emotionally charged as children's television and the profits from advertising to children.

It is not difficult to get the facts, but make sure that you do.

1.) Watch television. That sounds pretty obvious, but it is

surprising how many people—while alleging that there is nothing wrong—really have not sat down and looked at any television programs. Choose a specific program or time period that you want to watch. Find a clock with a second hand, some paper, and a pencil and while you watch, take notes on whatever aspect of the programing you might be interested in. A recent study of minorities in children's programing was based on careful viewing of fourteen and a half hours of Saturday children's programs in which every incident, character, and advertisement was noted down and later analyzed. It is also important to watch a program more than once. Series change week by week and while one story line may be offensive, the next week's program may be quite different.

You might design a simple form for monitoring programs with columns for the time of the program, description, and comments. For reference, you should always note the date, station, title of program, and producer which are usually given at the end of the program. (See the ACT Monitoring Form on p. 118.)

When monitoring, it is important to have a clock with a second hand since television programing is so segmented with interruptions for ads, announcements, promos, station identification, and introductions and closings of programs. In one half-hour, you may have twenty different items to note, as well as the content of the program segments.

You might decide to time and note the content of ads. Or you might write down a description of every event during the course of an hour's programing. You might prefer to watch a weekly series over a period of time or a daily series over a period of weeks.

Watching television with your child is the only way to apply what you have read in this book. Otherwise you will know no more about children's television than you would know about a painting from the artist's verbal description.

It is also absolutely essential that when you write letters or make any criticisms of children's television you are talking from your own viewing experience. No criticism loses its validity more quickly than one in which the complainant admits, "Well, I didn't actually see the program but . . ."

ACT MONITORING FORM

SHOW _____   **VIEWER** _____

STATION _____   **PHONE** _____

TIME _____   **DATE** _____

PRODUCER _____   **TYPE OF SHOW:** _____

Time	Commercial	Description of Program

INSTRUCTIONS FOR MONITORING

1. You will need: Monitoring form
                  Two pencils or pens
                  Clock or watch with a second hand
                  Take telephone off hook
                  Tune television in before program

2. Time the show from the beginning through the network break to the start of the next show.

3. Time the commercials accurately in minutes and seconds.
Use a clock or stopwatch with an easily visible second hand.
The commercials are usually thirty to sixty seconds long. There is no need to time the shows themselves.

4. For each ad, record the sponsor, product, and the length of the message. Add the total time and record in given space.

5. Give a brief synopsis of the story, stories, or other action in the program.

6. Use the back of the form for any additional comments.

7. Make a note of any period you stop monitoring during the program.

The following is a professional monitoring summary, showing children's television between 8:00 and 9:30 one Saturday morning on Channel 5 (WHDH-TV) in Boston. The symbols (PM, CA) refer to the segment timed (i.e., Program Material, Commercial Announcement, Noncommercial Announcement).

This was prepared by Dr. F. Earle Barcus of Boston University as part of his study *Saturday Children's Television*. Dr. Barcus timed seconds as percentages of a minute.

drawing by Susan

June 19, 1971, 8:00 A.M. to 9:30 A.M.

BUGS BUNNY/ROADRUNNER HOUR

			Minutes
8:00:00	PM	"Bugs Bunny/Roadrunner Hour" (Intro.)	1.75
8:01:45	CA	(Kool Aid)	.50
8:02:15	CA	(Kool Pop)	.50
8:02:45	PM	"Bunker Hill Bunny" (Cartoon)	6.67
8:09:25	CA	(Romper Room's Inchworm Toy)	.50
8:09:55	CA	(Grape Tang)	.50
8:10:25	PM	(Roadrunner Song and Chase) (Transition)	.42
8:10:50	CA	(General Mill's Count Chocula Cereal)	.50
8:11:20	CA	(General Mill's Cheerio's)	.50
8:11:50	PM	"Tweety's Circus" (Cartoon)	6.57
8:18:25	CA	(Keebler's Cookies)	.50
8:18:55	CA	(Keebler's Cookies)	.50
8:19:25	PM	"Bugs Bunny/Roadrunner Hour" (Transition)	.42
8:19:50	CA	(Mattel's Dawn Doll)	.50
8:20:20	CA	(Mattel's Zoomer Boomer)	.50
8:20:50	PM	"Gee Whizz" (Cartoon)	5.83
8:26:40	CA	(Post Sugar Crisp)	.50
8:27:10	CA	(Kool Pop)	.50
8:27:40	PM	"Stay tuned for part two" (Transition)	.42
8:28:05	NCA	"Keep Boston Clean"	.17
8:28:15	CA	(Birdseye Libbyland Frozen Dinners)	1.00
8:29:15	ID	"WHDH-TV" (VO); "Lassie" as visual	.08
8:29:20	PM	"Bugs Bunny/Roadrunner Hour" (Transitional)	.50
8:29:50	CA	(Kellogg's Raisin Bran)	.50
8:30:20	PM	"Hare Ways to the Stars" (Cartoon)	6.25
8:36:35	CA	(Nestles Quik)	.50
8:37:05	CA	(Nestles $100,000 Bar)	.50
8:37:35	PM	"Bugs Bunny/Roadrunner Hour" (Transitional)	.50
8:38:05	CA	(General Mill's Cheerio's)	.50
8:38:35	CA	(Kenner's SST Racer)	.50
8:39:05	PM	"Highway Runnery" (Cartoon)	6.00
8:45:05	CA	(Hershey Bars)	.50
8:45:35	CA	(Old Spice for Father's Day)	.50
8:46:05	PM	"Bugs Bunny/Roadrunner Hour" (Transitional)	.50
8:46:35	CA	(General Mill's Count Chocula/Frankenberry)	1.00
8:47:35	PM	"Bonanza Bunny" (Cartoon)	5.84
8:53:25	CA	(Quaker Cereals—Willy Wonka premium)	1.00
8:54:25	Promo	"Groovie Ghoulies and Sabrina"	.33
8:54:45	PM	"Bugs Bunny/Roadrunner Hour" (Visuals, Credits)	1.08
8:55:50	NCA	(Seat Belts)	.33

IN THE KNOW

8:56:10	PM	"In the Know"—"by Kellogg's"	.33
8:56:30	CA	(Kellogg's Rice Krispies)	.50
8:57:00	PM	"In the Know"—"Saturday in Rome"	1.68
8:58:40	Promo	(Captain Kangaroo) (CBS)	.33
8:59:00	CA	(McDonald's)	.50
8:59:30	NCA	(Boys' Club of America)	.50

THE GROOVIE GHOULIES AND SABRINA THE TEENAGE WITCH

9:00:00	ID	"WHDH-TV Boston" (Identification)	.08
9:00:05	PM	"Groovie Ghoulies . . ." (Jokes a la Laugh-In)	2.42
9:02:30	PM	"Hansel and Gretel" (Cartoon)	2.67
9:05:10	PM	"Horrible Horrorscope" (Cartoon)	2.08
9:07:15	CA	(General Mill's Count Chocula Cereal)	.50
9:07:45	CA	(Tang)	.50
9:08:15	PM	"Don't go away" (Transition)	.50
9:08:45	CA	(Romper Room's Inchworm Toy)	.50
9:09:15	CA	(General Mills' Count Chocula/Frankenberry)	.50
9:09:45	PM	"Beach Party" (Cartoon)	3.58
9:13:20	CA	(Pillsbury's Funny Face)	.50
9:13:50	CA	(Stuckey's—"Happy Highways' premium)	.50
9:14:20	PM	"Stick around" (Transition)	.33
9:14:40	CA	(Kellogg's Special K)	.50
9:15:10	CA	(Kellogg's Frosted Mini-Wheat)	.50
9:15:40	PM	"Beach Party" (Continued)	5.42
9:21:05	PM	"Don't go away" (Transition)	.33
9:21:25	CA	(Mattel's Dawn Doll and Friends)	.50
9:21:55	CA	(Shasta Soda)	.25
9:22:10	CA	(Burger King)	.50
9:22:40	PM	"Noises are the Strangest Things in the World" (Song)	2.67
9:25:20	CA	(Quaker Cereals—Willy Wonka premium)	1.00
9:26:20	PM	"Don't go away" (Transition)	.58
9:26:55	Promo	"The Week Ends Here"	.25
9:27:10	CA	(Spokies)	.50
9:27:40	CA	(McDonalds)	.50
9:28:10	ID	"WHDH-TV Boston" (Visual Red Sox)	.09
9:28:15	PM	"Stick around" (Transition)	.42
9:28:40	CA	(Sizzler's Fat Track)	.50
9:29:15	PM	"Weird Window Time" (Jokes a la Laugh-In)	3.34

2.) In order to keep informed about children's TV, read books and current magazines. Many newspapers have a daily TV column which is worth reading. The Resource Directory includes a bibliography on children's television.

COOPERATION

If you want to bring about real change, it is difficult to do it alone. If you can get together with a few friends, a local group, or an organization, you stand a much better chance of making waves and bringing about valid changes. That is how Action for Children's Television began.

Now an established national organization, ACT began one

winter evening in 1968 at a meeting in a suburban living room. A group of parents—some involved with the PTA and local groups—met to discuss children's television. From that meeting, initially concerned with television violence, a core committee of four women was formed, which spent weeks formulating a reasonable set of guidelines for children's TV. ACT has attracted a national membership and support from every state and has:

- • • educated professionals working with children to the significance of television and its influence on the young;
- • • established a National Resource Center on children and the media for use by educators and broadcasters;
- • • published a national Newsletter, sent to thousands of members and supporters;
- • • produced a film, *But First This Message*, showing exactly what network TV offers children and why.
- • • commissioned a study of Saturday morning children's television which found 71 percent of program content to be violent and 25 percent of program time devoted to commercials;
- • • commissioned a study analyzing black and minority treatment on children's TV;
- • • commissioned a study of the economic characteristics and alternate financing methods of children's TV;
- • • testified at government hearings on the effects of TV violence and commercialism on children;
- • • petitioned the Federal Communications Commission to eliminate commercialism from children's programs and stimulated an FCC inquiry into this area;
- • • petitioned the Federal Trade Commission to stop the selling of toys, edibles, and drugs directly to children on television;
- • • persuaded three major drug companies to withdraw their ads for vitamin pills from children's programs;
- • • sponsored three national conferences on children and television in cooperation with 1) Kennedy Memorial Hospital and Boston University School of Public Communication, 2) the American Academy of Pediatrics, and 3) Yale University Child Study Center and Yale School of Art;
- • • held an International Festival of Children's Television at the Kennedy Center, Washington, D.C.

In 1970, when Dean Burch was Chairman of the Federal Communications Commission, he said in a major speech:

Let me acknowledge the powerful influence of ACT on the prevailing climate of opinion. . . . ACT has gone to the core issue. They are asking, in effect, whether a commercially based broadcasting system is capable of serving up quality programing for an audience so sensitive and malleable as children.

ACT now has a board of advisors with a wide range of experiences and backgrounds, and its Resource Library is proving to be a gold mine of materials for those interested in this area, providing educational services such as a films, reprints of materials, speakers, and consultations as part of its work.

Local Groups and What They Can Do

ACT has never set up any chapters but encourages local groups to form their own "Committee on Children's Television" as independent units to deal with local problems in children's television. ACT has contacts in some fifty cities and towns, and the list is constantly expanding. ACT provides assistance and information but in no way dictates policy or direction for local groups. Perhaps you might like to set up a committee in your area or find out if one is already being set up. (See Resource Directory for list of ACT contacts.)

Every area has different television, depending upon the caliber of its program managers and station owners. For example, Boston has very different programing today from what it had ten years ago. One reason is that the local noncommercial public TV station has become a strong and popular force in the community, with a devoted viewing audience. The second is that, in an unprecedented license challenge case, the license of a VHF station was given to a new group of owners who have made great efforts to upgrade local programing. And third, is the presence in the Boston community of citizen groups, including ACT, concerned about programing.

The best thing a local group can do is to provide a sounding board for community ideas and interests and a source of information. At a preliminary meeting, for example, an open discussion of what is good or bad about local television might pinpoint some specific issues, i.e., no children's programs in the late afternoon, no programs for a large minority group within the community, an excessive number of reruns of old violent programs, etc. Or the interest of the group might lead it to choose to examine one specific area: for example, programing for Spanish-speaking viewers or for the deaf. The group could then decide the kind of action it would like to be involved in, beginning, perhaps, with letters to the stations, meetings with local program managers, articles in local newspapers, and discussions with other interested community leaders.

In Dayton, Ohio, two women have become involved in the local discussions about cable TV and children's programing in order to ensure that the promise of cable does not turn into another disaster area for children's television.

The Australian Children's Television Action Committee, devoted to upgrading children's TV and eliminating commercialism, conducted a survey to determine parents' concerns about children's programing. Aside from specific complaints, such as insufficient programing for school-age children, unpredictability of episodes in series, lack of Australian influence, and commercialism, parents expressed a need for education and public discussion.

Local committees on children's television can have far-reaching impact on the local broadcasting situation. Few broadcasters have any real knowledge of children, of child development, or of how television affects children. They respond to community comment. If a responsible local group can show a local broadcaster that it is to his advantage, as well as to the benefit of the child audience, to program the best and most interesting programs that he can find, then he is more inclined to do so. It is essential for him to know that if he does make an effort, his attempts will be noticed and commented upon. Don't complain bitterly about a poor quality program being offered to children in your community and then forget to thank the broadcaster when he replaces it with an excellent series of children's films.

What Effects Can Pressure Have?

Pressure and public comment can certainly have an effect on some aspects of children's television. Some broadcasters will ignore all criticisms and suggestions, but often broadcasters are ready to discuss criticisms and listen to ideas for improvement. Most efforts for change, however, take time and dedication.

In Boston, in September 1969, the local CBS outlet cut off the network program "Captain Kangaroo" halfway through the show. They ran a local children's show in the second half-hour. "Captain Kangaroo" was the only children's program available at that hour in Boston, and many parents called ACT to suggest that something be done. Several courses of action were taken:

1. Letters were written to the station by ACT, and other parents were urged to write to the station and local newspapers.
2. Two ACT members met with the general manager of the TV station and his assistant. The broadcasters explained that the expansion of their morning news show necessitated cutting the "Captain Kangaroo" hour. ACT was not convinced; the station ran several other news programs but did not have a single minute of children's programing at other times of the day.
3. ACT organized a "Good Natured Picket for Good Television" outside the station, with placards asking for "Captain Kangaroo—All of You," candy canes, balloons, and a girl with a guitar.
4. The station sent out a two-page letter to all who wrote in, explaining the cut. This backfired, since many parents were furious at the longwinded explanations and urged their friends and relatives to write in protesting the cut.

In January 1970, after thirteen weeks, the station reinstated the full hour of "Captain Kangaroo." ACT's efforts were credited with the restoration of the program.

Any effort to bring about a change in children's television must:

· · · have a clearly focused objective, which is limited in scope
· · · be planned carefully, so that you know what to expect
· · · be reasonable in demanding changes
· · · be properly researched and backed up with indisputable facts
· · · be legal
· · · be representative of the community, not just one individual

What Some Groups Have Done

Some groups are already involved in improving local children's television. San Francisco has a thriving Committee on Children's Television with a large, ethnically diverse board of advisors. The committee meets with local stations, is involved with the license challenge of one local station, and has become a visible force for upgrading children's television within the community.

When members of the local Chinese community were offended by a cartoon show depicting the Chinese in a derogatory way, they lodged a protest through the Committee on Children's Television. This resulted in several discussions, and plans for replacing the offending program with a show designed for Chinese children were put into motion. The show was taken off the Saturday morning schedule that spring, not rerun during the summer, and not scheduled as a network program the next season. But the station still has not provided a program specifically designed for Chinese children.

In a long-standing interchange with "Romper Room," the preschool program produced locally but with syndicated scripts and materials, ACT persuaded the owners of the program (Hasbro Toys) to stop the close involvement of the program's teacher with selling products, and to expand the content material of the show. This took three years, a thirty-five-page analysis of one week's programs, and a legal filing with the FCC, as well as several meetings with those involved.

A series of meetings between Citizens United for Responsive Broadcasting (CURB) and broadcasters in the New Orleans area in 1973 led to commitments by three stations to upgrade programs and commercials, including major changes for children's television. WDSU-TV agreed to continue to commit time and effort to presenting quality programs for children. In locally produced children's programs, WVUE-TV agreed to try to cluster commercials and to use children representing all segments of the community. WWL-TV, which already broadcasts "Captain Kangaroo," "You Are There," and the monthly "Spotlight on Youth," plans a half-hour weekly local children's program and agreed to eliminate commercials during children's programs that are offensive, misleading, or excessively hard-sell. This station is also establishing an advisory council with six members chosen from nominees of CURB, which will meet regularly.

In October 1973 KTTV, a Los Angeles Metromedia television station, agreed to ban forty-two violent programs and movies shown before 8:30 P.M. that contain excessive violence or horror. The warning consists of a slide with the words "Caution to Parents" and an announcer's voice saying: "Parents, we wish to advise that because of violence (or other possibly harmful elements) certain portions of the following program may not be suitable for young children."

The agreement was reached between KTTV and a coalition of four citizen's groups headed by the National Association for Better Broadcasting who filed a petition to deny the station's license two years ago.

Another precedent-setting agreement was signed in September 1973 between the licensee of WJIM-TV and the Lansing (Michigan) Committee for Children's Television (LCCT) and Citizens United for Better Broadcasting (CUBB). This followed from the formation of CUBB, several discussions with the station, and a petition to deny WJIM-TV's license.

Highlights of the agreement are:

1. A local daily half-hour children's show will begin within a year.
2. A local hour-long monthly special featuring the young people of the community will begin in January 1974.
3. WJIM-TV will develop local public service announcements featuring events, programs of interest, and needs of children in the WJIM service area.
4. Three representatives of LCCT will be included on the WJIM-TV Public Service Advisory Board.
5. A subcommittee on children's television will be formed which will include five members of LCCT's Advisory Board and/or LCCT members. It will assist WJIM in selection of syndicated programs for the late afternoon and early evening hours, with their important child-audience, and consult with WJIM on any locally produced children's programing. The committee will meet at least once every three months.
6. "Wild, Wild West" will be removed from the 5-6 P.M. time slot by January 1974 or earlier.
7. WJIM will experiment with the clustered ad concept on the proposed local daily children's show.

The agreement with the local citizens group became part of the station's official file at the Federal Communications Commission in Washington, D.C. The full text is included in the Resource Directory.

Suggestions for Forming a Group

If you would like to try cooperating with some other people, it is often best to set up some informal meeting at which you might show the ACT film *But First, This Message* or watch some television programs for children, or even look at some videotapes, which someone could make of children's television programs and commercials. Then, perhaps, encourage a general discussion and see what happens. The meeting might decide to set up a committee, with chairman, treasurer, and director, and with a definite plan of action and future meetings. Or it might simply be a philosophical talk about what television is doing to children and what it could be doing. Or it might be a place for parents to air their gripes about local programs, or discuss how they cope with TV watching in their homes. Or, it could be a good place to publicize programs worth looking out for or programs to avoid.

Try to leave the meeting reasonably open unless there is some clear local issue that urgently needs attention, and examine the mood of the participants. In some areas, the cancelation of a popular program may bring out a highly motivated group of viewers determined to work for its return. This can be an excellent basis for beginning a constructive group effort.

In many cases, the most constructive avenue is to set up a carefully scheduled monitoring program for one specific program or one specific time period, with two people watching each program daily, or weekly, over a short period of time. This can provide invaluable raw material for further action and discussion.

Whatever you do to encourage interest within your community is really "consciousness-raising" for those who participate since it will increase their awareness of how much influence television does have in the lives of our children.

Appendix:
From Guide to Citizen Action in Radio and Television

In Chapter 9 you read about community groups which have been involved in legal action in broadcasting. This included challenging the license of a TV station, filing a Petition to Deny, and initiating discussions with broadcasters. For those who would like to get involved, we have included here the details of more complicated legal actions citizens can take, extracted from an excellent booklet, *Guide to Citizen Action in Radio and Television*, by Marsha O'Bannon Prowitt, published by the Office of Communication, United Church of Christ, under a grant from The Markle Foundation in 1971. If you would like legal assistance in this area and are unable to find a local lawyer, try the Citizens Communications Center in Washington, D.C., the Office of Communication, United Church of Christ in New York City, or the Community Relations Service of the U.S. Department of Justice in Washington, D.C., who may be able to provide some legal advice and assistance. *A Public Citizen's Action Manual* by Donald K. Ross* gives valuable information about how to organize citizens action groups which could be applied to the area of children's broadcasting.

* New York: Grossman, 1973. With an Introduction by Ralph Nader.

All the following suggestions demand a great deal of time and involvement in terms of financial and professional commitment, and need serious consideration and research before you start to undertake them.

*   *   *

[It is important to know first the requirements or "Standards" the FCC has set for evaluating broadcasting service. Those that might apply to children's programing are discussed in section 1.]

1. FCC STANDARDS FOR PROGRAMING AND PERFORMANCE

REQUIREMENTS FOR PUBLIC PARTICIPATION IN PROGRAM PLANNING

When a broadcaster plans what programs his station will produce or carry each year, he is committed, by FCC rules, to involve the public . . . his audience . . . in what is known as *"contributive planning."* In explaining this responsibility, the FCC charged each licensee with *"finding his own path* [for programing] *with the guidance of those whom his signal is to serve."*

To discover this *"path,"* the Commission proposed that broadcasters begin by:

first, a canvass of the listening public . . . and
second, consultation with leaders in community life.

These consultations should include both leaders of community organizations and members of the general public. The prime criterion for these conferences is that the community leaders consulted must represent a true *cross-section* of the community, not just one or two majority interests.

In conducting his consultations and public canvass, the broadcaster must follow the guidelines contained in the FCC's *Primer on Ascertainment of Community Problems by Broadcast Licensees*. You may request a free copy from the FCC.

Periodically, the broadcasters must report to the FCC on these consultations, detailing with whom they have talked, what problems were identified, and what programing is planned to meet these community needs. The broadcaster must include very specific information on these consultations and programing promises in Section IV of his license renewal application.*. . .

If you look at the information included in Section IV of the license renewal form for stations in your community, and examine the additional exhibits the broadcaster has attached to his application to support his claims, you can find out:

- · · · If the broadcaster's list of community leaders and local citizens include leaders from the organizations and interests you support in your community.
- · · · If all the major interest groups in your community have been consulted in depth.
- · · · If the consultations reflect the broad spectrum of the community, including minority groups, young people, the poor, and people representing children's interest.
- · · · If the needs and interests set out by the broadcaster cover what you consider to be the real needs and interests of your community.
- · · · If the programs shown or heard in the past and those being planned by the broadcaster are responsible to these needs and interests.

* When applying for renewal of its license every three years, a station must file an "Application for Renewal" with the FCC at least ninety days before its license expires. This contains a mass of information important for evaluating the station's past programing and future promises and is available for public inspection either in the local community (usually at the station) or at the FCC office in Washington, D.C.

FCC POLICY ON PROGRAMING

The programing a broadcaster does has always been a primary indicator of his service to his public—and his right to hold a license. The FCC's basic programing policy statement identifies fourteen categories of programing that a station should carry as *"the major elements usually necessary to meet the public interest, needs, and desires of the community in which the station is located."* These categories are:

1. Opportunity for local expression
2. Development and use of local talent
3. Programs for children
4. Religious programs
5. Educational programs
6. Public Affairs programs
7. Editorialization by licensees
8. Political broadcasts
9. Agricultural programs
10. News programs
11. Weather and market reports
12. Sports programs
13. Service to minority groups
14. Entertainment programs

While the FCC does not require a broadcaster to offer a particular percentage of programing in any of these categories, the Commission has stated that a station must offer a balanced program schedule that meets the needs and interests of *all* substantial groups in his audience. These program categories can be helpful to you in assessing whether broadcasters in your community are providing a "balanced" program diet for their listeners.

The difference between what the station is actually doing and what the FCC says it *should* be doing can provide you with a valuable yardstick on broadcaster performance in your area.

One point that the FCC and the courts have made time and time again is that the profitability (or lack of it) in carrying certain types of programing bears little relation to the broadcaster's obligation to provide it to this audience. Obviously, under the current system of free enterprise in broadcasting no official or unofficial body can or would issue rulings that would drive a broadcaster to bankruptcy. But stations cannot deny public service programing strictly on the basis that it cannot find sponsors to handle its cost. It is inherent in the public responsibility sections of their license that public service programing must be part of their program schedules, whether it is sponsored or not. Economically, at that point, it is not a question of the stations losing money. It is simply a problem of their not squeezing the maximum amount of profit out of the broadcast day.

In the important Red Lion case in 1969, the U.S. Supreme Court stated that *"it is the right of the public to receive suitable access to social, political, esthetic, moral and other ideas and experience . . . in programing."* And the fulfillment of that broadcaster responsibility is on the record for you to see. Station license renewal forms must specifically include:

· · · lists of proposed programs designed to respond to community needs and interests,
· · · lists of past programs broadcast to fulfill community needs and interests,
· · · news staff and program time for local and regional news,
· · · past and proposed program formats,
· · · an evaluation of station contribution to overall diversity of program services available in your community,
· · · number of public service announcements broadcast weekly,
· · · network affiliation,
· · · time and percentage of programing in news, public affairs, and "other" programing (excluding entertainment and sports).

THE "FAIRNESS" STANDARD IN BROADCASTING

The presentation of news and public affairs programing is probably the single most important public service a radio or television station can render to its community. A broadcaster has special and continuing responsibility for fairness in this area; fairness in the handling of controversial issues of public importance, fairness in the handling of people running for public office. Over the years, the rules governing his actions in this sensitive area have become known as "The Fairness Doctrine."

To meet his obligations, the broadcaster has to fulfill two basic requirements:

• • • First, he must broadcast discussions of issues of great public concern;

• • • Second, he must assure overall fairness in that discussion by giving fair coverage to each substantial viewpoint on an issue.

Furthermore, broadcasters must program to meet their fairness obligations at their own expense if paid sponsorship is unavailable and must seek out spokesmen of contrasting views if none volunteer.

The fairness requirement in broadcasting is one of our most precious public rights. It is intended to promote debate of public issues and to force broadcasters into using their stations as forums for the exchange of ideas and views. A broadcaster is not fulfilling his responsibility if he presents only bland and non-controversial programing or if he monopolizes the programing with only one side, or his view, of an important issue.

Some of the issues that have been considered as "controversial issues of public importance" by the FCC are civil rights, labor disputes, health food fads, pay TV and CATV, school desegregation, and U.S. foreign aid. These are national issues generally, although with local application. But important *local* issues fall under the doctrine as well. The rule-of-thumb criteria for local Fairness Doctrine application may be interpreted as issues that affect a major part of the community and that have elements of the community on different sides of the question.

Once again, the Supreme Court recently backed the public in this broadcast issue. The Court rejected arguments by broadcasters that the Fairness Doctrine discouraged the programing of controversial matters and interfered with freedom of speech because the Doctrine required stations to provide time for all sides to speak. In its opinion, the Supreme Court said:

It does not violate the First Amendment to treat licensees given the privilege of using scarce radio frequencies as proxies for the entire community, obligated to give suitable time and attention to matters of great public concern. To condition the granting or renewal of licenses on a willingness to present representative community views on controversial issues is consistent with the ends and purposes of those constitutional provisions forbidding the abridgement of freedom of speech and freedom of the press. (Supreme Court, Red Lion, 1969.)

Keep in mind that a reasonable opportunity for all sides to discuss conflicting views does not require that equal time be given for each argument. Overall station programing and not a single program or program series is the test for compliance with fairness. The broadcaster has considerable discretion as to the technique, format, or spokesman he may choose to comply with the ruling.

Several individuals and citizen groups have tried to get the FCC to apply the requirements of the Fairness Doctrine to commercials that present one viewpoint on controversial issues of public importance, such as pollution and drug usage. With the exception of cigarette commercials (which were later outlawed by act of Congress), the Commission has ruled that the Fairness Doctrine is not applicable to product advertising—even when the claims made relate to a matter of public concern. The Commission has announced an inquiry of the Fairness Doctrine which includes this issue. . . .

EQUAL EMPLOYMENT STANDARDS

The FCC recently adopted sweeping new rules that require all commercial and noncommercial stations to establish programs designed to eliminate discrimination in station employment.

The rules charge the stations with developing *"positive recruitment, training, job design and other measures in order to insure genuine equality of opportunity to participate fully in all organizational units, occupations and levels of responsibility in the station."*

The Commission further stated specific practices each station *must* follow in recruitment, selection, training, placement, promotion, pay, working conditions, demotion, layoff, and termination. They also suggested that broadcasters *"might consider the adoption of special training programs for qualifiable minority group members, [and] cooperative action with other organizations to improve employment opportunities and community conditions that affect employability. . . ."*

Stations must report regularly to the FCC on their progress in implementing these new rules. An annual report must be submitted by May 31 detailing statistics on station employment of blacks, Orientals, American Indians, Spanish-surnamed Americans, and women. In addition, at license renewal time, broadcasters must henceforth report in a new Section VI of their application the specific practices they are following to secure equal employment at all levels in their station. (The only exceptions to this new reporting are stations with less than five employees.)

COMMERCIALS AND ADVERTISING

Commercial radio and television is an advertiser-supported medium. The money derived by the station selling time to advertisers provides broadcasters with the funds to buy and produce programs and, of course, with their profits. The only product prohibited from advertising on radio and TV is cigarettes.

The FCC long ago accepted advertising as necessary to the economic support of broadcast operations, but has warned broadcasters that they must not let commercial interests drive out their public interest responsibilities. Nevertheless, it will take extraordinary efforts by the public to insure that the programing needs of the public always take priority over the commercial interests of advertisers and broadcasters.

Broadcaster Responsibility for Advertising Material

The FCC has stated flatly that stations must assume responsibility for all programing—including commercials—that they broadcast. In its programing policy statement of 1960, the Commission said:

With respect to advertising material, the licensee has the additional responsibility to take all reasonable measures to eliminate any false, misleading or deceptive matter and to avoid abuses with respect to the total amount of time devoted to advertising continuity as well as the frequency with which regular programs are interrupted for advertising messages.

To underscore their point, the FCC added that responsibility for all these commercial criteria *"is personal to the licensee and may not be delegated."* The FCC *does* consider advertising an important public interest function of the station, so you can also use it as one of the criteria by which you evaluate a station's performance in your community.

The FCC cannot regulate commercials for taste or propriety. Those are matters of editorial judgment and not within the Commission's province. That is not to say *you* as citizens cannot protest to your station about these things. But your power is that of a customer protesting how you're being treated by a salesman, not as a citizen backed by law.

2. NON-LEGAL ACTION

["Complaints" and "PR, Letter, and Education Campaigns" are discussed in Chapter 9.]

BOYCOTTS

Questions about the usefulness of boycotts against objectionable station programs are frequently raised. One piece of information should put into perspective the questionable nature of this tactic: stations have the advantage of being able to measure the effectiveness of any boycott through the information they receive from their rating services—information that you cannot get.

COMMUNITY NEGOTIATION WITH STATIONS

It is possible for well organized and representative community groups to negotiate with radio and television stations and obtain significant improvement in service. Based on past experience, this kind of action must be supported by a substantial number of people and organizations in the community, it must root proposed reforms substantially in the law, it must be supported by careful research and observation of the media, and it must have the assistance of attorneys briefed in communications law. The key to a successful negotiation effort between community groups and station management is the ability and readiness to take legal action against the station—usually in the form of a Petition to Deny its license renewal—if efforts to reach a satisfactory local settlement fail.

While this type of effort requires extraordinary organization, research, and work for a period of three to five months and sustained interest thereafter, groups in a number of cities, including Dallas, Atlanta, Chicago, and Nashville, have won significant reforms in station performance in their cities and believe the benefits well worth the effort. Such reforms have included new training programs, scholarships and employment for minority persons, regularly scheduled consultations with community groups to discuss policies and programing, increased news coverage of black community events, public service spot campaigns about community problems, institution of procedures to screen advertising for demeaning reference to ethnic and racial groups, development of programing of special interest to the black community, additional children's programs, public affairs and consumer information programs and announcements.

Agreements vary from community to community as they reflect circumstances and needs in each city. Predominantly black and, recently, Chicano groups who have documented discrimination in employment and programing have been most vigirous and effective in using this negotiation route to improved broadcast services.

3. LEGAL ACTION

You may want to consider filing an objection or Petition to Deny the station renewal of license. The explanation of these legal procedures will seem complex, but do not be discouraged.

Community groups throughout the nation, aided by attorneys, have been successful in using them. Experienced national organizations can also offer you guidance in these undertakings.

The Petition to Deny is the most severe action a citizen group can take against a broadcast station. Such petitions are costly and extremely time consuming to both the petitioner and the broadcaster. It should be considered the last resort when other means of achieving necessary change in local broadcast service have failed. A citizen group will need to have expert legal assistance prior to filing a petition.

The most severe penalty the FCC can impose is denial of the applicant's license—but levy of other penalties, such as fines and short-term renewals, is also appropriate. In the past renewals have been denied broadcast stations on public interest grounds including overcommercialization, serious and repeated violations of the Fairness Doctrine, fraud, and consistent racial discrimination in programing.

Citizen groups have used a Petition to Deny license renewal where broadcasters willfully and consistently flout the public interest. . . .

In 1964, the Office of Communication, United Church of Christ, joined by two black civil rights leaders in the Jackson, Mississippi community, filed a Petition to Deny license renewal of station WLBT-TV on the grounds that the station discriminated against the interests of the black community which represented 45 percent of its viewers. After years of legal action before the FCC and in the courts, the U.S. Court of Appeals in 1969 revoked the license of the station. A precedent won for all of us in this long fight is the right of the public to be heard and to have our views made part of the official record in license renewal proceedings. . . .

Petition to Deny

A Petition to Deny begins with an explanation of why you are a "party of interest." A broadly based citizen group should have no difficulty establishing that it qualifies under this definition. The petition next sets out the "allegations of fact"—the issues in the case. If, for example, one of your charges is that the station discriminates against minority people in its employment, you should support this allegation with *specific* information which might include statistics on the low employment of minority people in each category of station responsibility as compared with population of minority groups in the city or of minority people who have applied for employment; signed statements (affidavits) of minority persons who have been denied employment, citing specific violations of the equal employment rules and other relevant material.

Attach to the Petition to Deny as exhibits, signed and notarized statements of persons who have personal knowledge of the charges you have made against a station and any relevant monitoring analysis or special research studies you have conducted. Hearsay, rumor, opinion, or broad generalizations are not acceptable. The more thoroughly documented your allegations, the better chance you will have that the FCC will seriously consider your petition and that penalties or corrective action will result.

A Petition to Deny must be filed no later than the first day of the last full month of the license period and a copy served on the applicant. After you have filed your petition, the broadcaster is allowed ten days in which to file an "Opposition to the Petition to Deny." The petitioning citizen group is then allowed five days in which to file a "Reply to the Opposition." The Reply to the Opposition allows the petitioner an opportunity to further support his original allegations, as well as to counter whatever allegations the station offers to defend itself.

If the FCC decides that your petition raises substantial public interest questions about a broadcaster, it will set the application for hearing on the issues you have raised. If you wish the hearing to be held in your community you should make that request in your petition.

In several instances the submission of a well-researched and documented Petition to Deny has moved the affected station to reconsider reforms or changes heretofore considered unacceptable. Agreement has often been reached after a petition has been filed. In several cases the written agreement was forwarded to the FCC as an amendment to the license renewal application and the citizen group withdrew its petition.

Much greater detail on the requirements of a Petition to Deny and the subsequent hearing are included in a booklet available from the FCC, *The Public in Broadcasting: A Procedure Manual.* You should read the sections relevant to the action you contemplate and follow the steps and requirements set out there.

Informal Objections

Another means of seeking FCC remedy to the objections a citizen group may have to a broadcaster's performance is an "Informal Objection." Informal Objections are not subject to the cut-off dates which apply to Petitions to Deny and may be filed at any time until the renewal of a station's license. Filings must be signed by the objector but there are no formal standards for content. However, as a practical matter, it is a good idea to follow the standards for a Petition to Deny and include a factual analysis of the station's application, together with concrete information supporting the charges. Include as many facts and figures as possible.

You may wish to consider filing an informal objection if the deadline for a Petition to Deny is fast approaching or past or if your citizen group feels that a Petition is unwarranted or if it is unable to assume the burdens of a formal legal action. This is also a useful mechanism for individuals wishing to have their objections to a broadcast renewal considered.

If the Commission concludes that a substantial and material question of fact has been presented or if it is for any reason unable to find that a grant of the application would serve the public interest, it will order a hearing. Otherwise it will grant renewal of the license.

PARTICIPATION IN OTHER APPLICATION PROCEEDINGS

Aside from license renewal, there are other times when citizen groups can enter legal objections to a Commission action affecting a station. Whenever the FCC has before it an application to grant, modify, or approve the sale of a broadcast station, it must make a specific determination that the public interest will be served. Therefore, public interest questions raised by citizen groups at these times have a great impact because substantial objections must be considered before the Commission can approve an action as in the "public interest."

When such applications are pending, individuals and citizen's groups may enter their objections in the same way as they can in license renewal proceedings: by complaint, by Petition to Deny the application, or by an Informal Objection. Basically the same ground rules as to form, content and filing deadlines apply in these situations as well.

At these times you may raise any public interest question relating to the application or the applicant. If, for example, the applicant is seeking to construct a new antenna tower, you might argue that the application should be denied because the station has engaged in discriminatory hiring practices. In other words, the issues raised need not relate directly to the construction of the tower. You may also support the application.

Frequently the very nature of the proposed change in facilities or ownership directly affects the public interest. For example, when the sale or transfer of a station is proposed, the buyer may wish to change the music or programing format of the station— or his ownership of other media properties may raise serious questions as to whether concentration of control of media would result to the detriment of the public. In these cases, negotiation may not hold the answers to citizen group objections and legal avenues of redress should be considered. You may gain important perspectives from the efforts and successes of other citizen groups who have participated in FCC proceedings involving the transfer or sale of stations. . . .

An . . . example of effective citizen action occurred in Atlanta, Georgia. The proposed sale of the only classical music station to a buyer who indicated he would change the music format to "middle of the road" spurred the formation of a citizen group of classical music lovers—the Citizen's Committee to Preserve the Voice of the Arts in Atlanta on WGKA-AM/FM. The Citizen's Committee petitioned the FCC for a hearing alleging that the musical interests of a substantial group in the Atlanta community would not be served by the sale. While the FCC denied their request, upon appeal, the U.S. Court of Appeals ordered the FCC to hold the hearing. The Court said that all substantial groups within a community have a right to service from the broadcast stations in their city:

> [I]t is surely in the public interest . . . for all major aspects of contemporary culture to be accommodated by the commonly owned public resources whenever that is technically and legally possible.

The Court went on to observe that the 16 percent of the residents of Atlanta who appear to prefer classical music are

> not an insignificant portion of the people who make up Atlanta; and their minority position does not exclude them from consideration in such matters as the allocation of radio channels for the greatest good for the greatest number.

In the hearing, the citizen group will try to demonstrate that the needs, tastes, and interests of the substantial group of classical music lovers in the Atlanta area, which they represent, will not be served adequately if the one station broadcasting classical music changes its format.

POTENTIAL FOR OPERATING A NEW STATION

Application for Vacant Channel

Any financially qualified U.S. individual, group, or corporation can apply for an available frequency (channel) to operate a commercial or noncommercial radio or television station. The FCC has a table of assignment of frequencies for FM radio stations and VHF and UHF television stations. Some channels are for commercial operation, others are set aside for noncommercial use. While there are very few unassigned channels for either radio or television stations in the major metropolitan areas, many possibilities remain for new stations in rural areas or small towns. There are many frequencies still available for noncommercial FM radio stations in these smaller communities.

If you wish to investigate the availability of frequencies in your area and the procedures necessary to apply, write the FCC and ask if there is an unassigned frequency for FM or TV stations, commercial or noncommercial, in your community. Ask for the FCC booklet, *How to Apply for a Broadcast License.*

In rare instances, broadcast licenses for existing stations are revoked by the FCC and are then available. There is an opportunity for other parties to submit application for the license to operate a new station. If you have the necessary resources, you might also consider hiring an engineering firm to determine if it is possible to move an unused frequency assigned elsewhere to your community or to determine if an AM channel could be located.

Comparative Hearings

When there is more than one applicant for the license of the same frequency (channel) the FCC holds a comparative hearing to judge the relative merits of the applicants. There are several standards and requirements the FCC has established by which to evaluate competing applicants. The basic standards are discussed in the *FCC Policy Statement on Comparative Broadcast Hearings.* Two primary objectives are: first, the best practicable service to the public; and, second, a maximum diffusion of control of the media of mass communications. A competing applicant must also demonstrate ability and experience in broadcasting, legal qualifications, and financial resources required for station operation. He must also ascertain community needs and propose a program service to meet them. . . .

Competing Applications for Existing Broadcast Licenses

Another much more difficult option is available to community groups. Because a broadcaster has been awarded his license to operate a station for a term of only three years, it is possible to submit a second, competing application for the license of an *existing* radio or television station when it is up for renewal. The qualification criteria and standards for broadcast applications and subsequent comparative hearings apply in these cases as well.

This type of action introduced a dynamic, competitive element into the existing system of broadcasting. But the difficult cost, expertise, and time required for such a competing application cannot be overemphasized. Only once in the history of broadcasting has a competing applicant been preferred over the present operator: the license for Channel 5 in Boston was awarded to one of four new applicants. Yet today new broadly based community corporations are competing for the licenses of TV stations in New York, Boston, and Washington, D.C.

Any party seriously considering filing a competing application should seek competent legal advice at least six months in advance of the deadline. Competing applications must be filed no later than the first day of the last full month of the license period.

PUBLIC PARTICIPATION IN FCC RULE MAKINGS

In order to be able to carry out its obligation to regulate radio and television broadcasting, the FCC has authority to issue rules *"as public convenience, interest, or necessity requires."* And there is opportunity for the public to participate in establishing and defining those rules that govern broadcasting.

Any interested party including an individual or citizen group may petition the FCC for the issuance, amendment, or repeal of a rule or regulation. Public parties may also submit their "Comments" on a new rule proposed by the Commission. These comments are weighed when the FCC is deciding whether to issue a new rule. Frequently the perspectives entered by public groups have had the effect of substantially changing the provisions of a proposed rule so that it more accurately takes into account the needs of the public.

To date, the establishment of rules has effectively been an interaction between broadcasters and the FCC. As a result, many rules reflect the broadcaster's viewpoint and do not take public needs into consideration. With the growing activism and sophistication of public groups, this practice is changing.

Not only is the public affecting rules proposed by the Commission but it is also initiating requests for new rules which may better serve the public interest as the public groups see it. . . .

Action for Children's Television petitioned the FCC for new rules which would limit the amount and commercial content of children's programing and set minimum requirements and recommended times for programing especially designed for various age groups of children. [*See* page 68.]

Many community groups have an interest in the rules that are proposed by the Commission regularly each week. It is not difficult to enter comments on a proposed rule. The cover page should cite the specific proposed rule, and be titled COMMENTS. You should then include arguments in support—or in opposition—of the proposed rule and any proposed modifications you may wish to have considered. The original and fourteen copies of these comments should be submitted to the Secretary of the FCC by the deadline set by the FCC.

While it is not difficult to submit comments in a rule-making proceeding, it is difficult to learn what new rules have been proposed. A layman or community group might subscribe to *Broadcasting* magazine which regularly reports FCC actions and applicable deadlines, then write the FCC for a copy of the Notice of Proposed Rulemaking.

Only groups with considerable experience in broadcasting should attempt to initiate new rules. A petition to the Commission for new rules should recite the proposed rule, the proposed amendment, or the section to be repealed. In addition, it should include arguments in support of the requested action and an explanation as to how the interests of the petitioner and the public would be affected thereby. If the Commission accepts your proposal, it will issue a Notice of Proposed Rulemaking and set deadlines for the submission of comments. After the rule making is closed, the FCC will determine what rule, if any, should be issued on the basis of the comments it has received and its own judgment.

4. PENALTIES

If a broadcaster fails to meet government standards for serving the public interest, the FCC has the power and the obligation to correct him. The most common of all Commission actions against a station is simply to order the violator to comply with whatever FCC decision or rule that is involved and set a date for compliance. There are several other economic and legal measures that can be taken by the FCC to insure compliance with the law:

- • • Denying a broadcaster's application for license renewal
- • • Revoking an existing license
- • • Granting a short-term renewal to see if a broadcaster will correct existing violations
- • • Assessing of a fine for violations
- • • Initiating a court action to force violators to "cease and desist" offensive practices. Continuing violations in the face of a court order can result in a broadcaster being jailed.

*   *   *

Resource Directory

USEFUL ADDRESSES

GOVERNMENT AGENCIES

Director, Consumer Product Information Center, Public Documents Distribution Center, Pueblo, Colorado 81009

Chairman, Consumer Product Safety Commission, 1750 K St. N.W., Washington, D.C.

Chairman, Federal Communications Commission, Washington, D.C. 20554

Chairman, Federal Trade Commission, Bureau of Consumer Protection, Washington, D.C. 20580

Director, Food and Drug Administration, Department of Health, Education, and Welfare, 303 Independence Ave., SW., Washington, D.C.

Director, Office of Telecommunications Policy, Executive Office of the President, Washington, D.C. 20504

Both the Senate and the House of Representatives have subcommittees responsible for television and communications. For your information, a complete list of members of those committees follows. Write to them at either the Senate Office Building or the House Office Building, Washington, D.C.

Senate Commerce Committee Subcommittee on Communications

John O. Pastore (D., R.I.), Chairman
Vance Hartke (D., Ind.), Vice Chairman
Howard H. Baker, Jr. (R., Tenn.)
J. Glenn Beall (R., Md.)
Howard W. Cannon (D., Nev.)
Marlow W. Cook (R., Ky.)
Robert P. Griffin (R., Mich.)
Philip A. Hart (R., Mich.)
Ernest R. Hollings (D., S.C.)
Daniel K. Inouye (D., Hawaii)
Russell B. Long (D., La.)
Frank F. Moss (D., Utah)
James B. Pearson (R., Kan.)
Theodore F. Stevens (R., Alaska)

House Interstate and Foreign Commerce Committee Subcommittee on Communications and Power

Torbert H. Macdonald (D., Mass.) Chairman
Clarence J. Brown, Jr. (R., Ohio)
Goodloe E. Byron (D., Md.)
James M. Collins (R., Texas)
Louis Frey, Jr. (R., Fla.)
Barry M. Goldwater, Jr. (R., Calif.)
John M. Murphy (D., N.Y.)
Fred B. Rooney (D., Pa.)
Lionel Van Deerlin (D., Calif.)

NETWORKS

Address your letters to the presidents of these companies.

ABC, 1330 Avenue of the Americas, New York, N.Y. 10019 (212-LT1-7777)

CBS, 51 West 52 St., New York, N.Y. 10019 (212-765-4321)

NBC, 50 Rockefeller Plaza, New York, N.Y. 10020 (212-CI7-8300)

PBS, 485 L'Enfant Plaza S.W., Washington, D.C. (202-488-5000)

STATION GROUPS

Some major groups owning television stations are listed below. Address your letters to the president.

Avco Broadcasting Corp., 1600 Provident Tower, Cincinnati, Ohio 45202

Capital Cities Broadcasting Corp., 24 E. 51 St., New York, N.Y. 10022

Cox Broadcasting Stations, 1602 W. Peachtree St. N.E., Atlanta, Ga. 30309

John E. Fetzer Stations, 590 W. Maple St., Kalamazoo, Mich. 49001

Forward Communications Inc., Box 1088, 1114 Grand Ave., Wausau, Wis. 54401

Hearst Stations, 959 Eighth Ave., New York, N.Y. 10019

Kaiser Broadcasting Stations, 300 Lakeside Drive, Kaiser Bldg., Oakland, Calif. 94604

Metromedia Inc., 277 Park Ave., New York, N.Y. 10017

Post-Newsweek, Broadway House, Washington, D.C. 20016

RKO General Inc., 1440 Broadway, New York, N.Y. 10018

Scripps-Howard Group, 200 Park Ave., New York, N.Y. 10017

Storer Broadcasting Co., 1177 Kane Concourse, Miami Beach, Fla. 33154

Taft Broadcasting Co., 1906 Highland Ave., Cincinnati, Ohio 45219

Tribune Co. (*Chicago Tribune*) Stations, 2501 Bradley Place, Chicago, Ill. 60618

Westinghouse Broadcasting Stations, 90 Park Ave., New York, N.Y. 10016

(Complete information available from Broadcasting Yearbook, 1735 DeSales Street N.W., Washington, D.C. 20036.)

LOCAL STATIONS

Every local television station has a call-sign beginning with "W" east of the Mississippi and with "K" west of the Mississippi. To find the addresses and phone numbers of your local stations, look up the call-signs in the phone book under "W" or "K" (WNEW, KRON, etc.). Address your letters to the president of the station.

ORGANIZATIONS AND GROUPS

Action for Children's Television, 46 Austin Street, Newtonville, Mass. 02160 (617-527-7870) National organization of parents and professionals, working to upgrade television for children and to eliminate commercialism from children's TV. Membership, newsletter, campaigns, research information, film, and library facilities.

Center for the Study of Responsive Law, P.O. Box 19367, Washington, D.C. 20036. Nader founded this group of lawyers who investigate a variety of areas in response to consumer needs. Provides legal advice, publishes books on areas studied.

Citizens Communications Center, 1812 N Street N.W., Washington, D.C. 20036. Provides legal assistance and advice to citizens interested in taking action in broadcasting area. Publishes annual report.

Council on Children, Media, and Merchandising, 1346 Connecticut Avenue N.W., Washington, D.C. 20036. The Council, created by Robert Choate, is most active in areas relating to nutrition and food advertising to children.

National Academy of Television Arts and Sciences, 54 W. 40 St., New York, N.Y. 10018. Professional organization of broadcast producers and performers. Publishes some materials.

National Association for Better Broadcasting, P.O. Box 130. Topanga, Calif. 90290. Oldest broadcasting organization. Has membership, publishes newsletter and annual critique of programs on the air.

National Association for the Education of Young Children (Media Committee, 1834 Connecticut Avenue N.W., Washington, D.C. 20009. Leading organization for teachers of preschool children; publishes journal and has special committee preparing materials about the media.

National Citizens Committee for Broadcasting, 1914 Sunderland Place N.W., Washington, D.C. 20036. Was active in 1960s and then lapsed. Now revitalizing as a national organization planning to coordinate all citizen efforts in broadcasting.

Office of Communication, United Church of Christ, 289 Park Ave. S., New York, N.Y. 10010. Dr. Everett Parker has made the Office of Communication a spearhead of legal efforts to improve minority representation in broadcasting. Publishes some materials, gives advice.

Urban Communications Group, 1730 M Street N.W., Washington, D.C. 20036. A group involved in minority ownership in broadcasting, especially cable TV.

ACT CONTACTS

There are individuals or committees concerned with children's television in the cities listed below. For more information about one in your area, write to ACT (46 Austin St., Newtonville, Mass. 02160).

Australia: MacLeod, Victoria
California: Canyon County, Riverside, San Francisco
Colorado: Denver
Connecticut: New Haven
Florida: Coral Gables, Winter Park
Georgia: Atlanta
Illinois: Evanston
Indiana: Indianapolis
Louisiana: New Orleans
Maine: Bangor
Maryland: Silver Springs
Massachusetts: Marblehead, Newton Center, Sudbury, Wellesley
Michigan: East Lansing, Huntington Woods
Mississippi: Jackson, University
Missouri: St. Louis, Warrensburg
Montana: Custer
New Hampshire: Weare
New Jersey: Cliffside Park, New Brunswick
New Mexico: Albuquerque, Fort Sumner
New York: Massapequa, New York City, Rochester
North Carolina: Chapel Hill
Ohio: Cincinnati, Cuyahoga Falls, Dayton, Lyndhurst
Pennsylvania: Chester, Pittsburgh
Rhode Island: Newport
South Carolina: Charleston
Texas: San Antonio, Dallas
Virginia: Reston
Washington: Mercer Island, Seattle
Washington, D.C.
Wisconsin: Madison

USEFUL ADDRESSES OUTSIDE USA

If you would like to find out information about children's television in other countries, the following addresses should provide a starting point for research.

Australia
Honorary Secretary, Australian Children's Television Action Committee, 70 Aberdeen Road, McLeod, Victoria, Australia 3085

Austria
Director, Ost. Rundfunk, A 1040 Wien/Osterreich, Aretntinierstr. 22, Austria

Belgium
Director of Children's Programs, Belgische Radio en TV, Blvd. Reyers, B 1040 Brussels, Belgium
Executive Secretary, EURNAC, Avenue de Tervuerene 265, 1150 Bruxelles, Belgium

Canada
National Program Director, CTV Television Network, 42 Charles Street East, Toronto, 285 Canada
President, Canadian Broadcasting Corporation, 1500 Bronson Ave., Toronto, Ont., Canada
Children's Program Division, Societe Radio-Canada (TV), 1400 Dorchester Blvd. East, Montreal, Canada
Chairman, Canadian Radio-TV Commission, 2nd floor/Berger Bldg., 100 Metcalfe Street, Ottawa, Ont., Canada
Director, Canadian Council on Children and Youth (Media Division), 242 St. George, Toronto, Canada
"Violence on TV" movie, Challenge for Change, National Film Board, P.O. Box 6100, Montreal 101, PQ, Canada

Czechoslovakia
Director of Programs, CTV, 16 Jindrisska, Prague, Czechoslovakia

Denmark
Director of Children's TV, Danmarks Radio-TV, Morkhojvej 170, D 2860 Soborg, Denmark

England
Children's Programing, BBC Television, Wood Lane, London W. 12, England
Director, Independent Television Authority (commercial TV), 70 Brompton Road, London S.W. 3, England

Finland
Director of Programing, YLE-Oy Yleisradio Ab, 0026 Helsinki 26, Finland

France
Director of Children's Programs, ORTF, 116 Av. du President Kennedy, F 75790 Paris, France

Germany
Director, Prix Jeunesse, Bayerischer Rundfunk, 8000 Munchen 2, Rundfunkplatz 1, Germany

Ghana
Director of Programs, Ghana Broadcasting Corporation, P.O. Box 1633, Accra, Ghana

Hungary
Director of Programs, MRTV, Szabadsag Ter 17, Budapest, Hungary

Iran
Director, National Iranian Radio and TV, P.O. Box 33-200, Tadrish, Pahlavi Road, Tehran, Iran

Israel
Children's and Youth Programs, Hebrew Programing, Israeli Television, Jerusalem, Israel

Japan
Director of Children's Programs, Radio and Television Research, Nippon Hoso Kyokai, 1-10, Atago-Cho, Shiba, Minato-Ku, Tokyo 105, Japan

Nigeria
Director of Children's Programs, Nigerian Broadcasting Company, Broadcasting House, Vitoria Island, Lagos, Nigeria

Norway
Director, Norsk Rikskringkasting, Oslo 3, Norway

Spain
Children's Dept., Television Española, Prado del Rey, Madrid, Spain

Sweden
Director of Programing, Sveriges Radio TV, 105 10 Stockholm, Sweden

International
Director, European Broadcasting Union, Centre International, 1 rue de Varembe, CH-1211 Geneva 20
Editor, World Radio-TV Handbook, Soliljevej 44, 2650 Hvidivre, Denmark

BIBLIOGRAPHY ON CHILDREN'S TELEVISION

MATERIALS AVAILABLE FROM ACT

ACT Speech to Prix Jeuness. Munich, Germany, October 1973. $2.00.

ACT Survival Kits: *Advice on Toys at Christmas* (ATAC), 25¢; *Turn off Television Saturday* (TOTS). 25¢. *Nutrition Survival Kit*, 25¢.

BARCUS, F. EARLE. *Concerned Parents Speak Out on Children's Television.* A Report on the ACT/Parade Magazine Quiz. Prepared for Action for Children's Television, March 1973. 95 pages, $10.00.

BARCUS, F. EARLE. *Romper Room: An Analysis.* Prepared for Action for Children's Television, September 1971. 35 pages, $5.00.

BARCUS, F. EARLE. *Saturday Children's Television: A Report of Television Programming and Advertising on Boston Commercial Television.* Prepared for Action for Children's Television, July 1971. 54 pages and Appendix, $10.00.

BARCUS, F. EARLE. *Network Programming and Advertising in the Saturday Children's Hours: A June and November Comparison.* An update of the above study, January 1972. 32 pages, $5.00.

But First, This Message. Prepared for Action for Children's Television by Cinemagraphics, Inc., 1971. A fifteen-minute, 16mm. color film with sound. Film Clips from children's TV programs. Statements from children, physicians, a toy manufacturer, a professor of communications, and a professor of child development. To rent: $25.00; to purchase: $100.00.

Federal Communication Commission Documents Filed by ACT-RM1569. (Charges to cover reprinting and mailing.) Brief I, *Guidelines for Children's Television.* April 29, 1970. $5.00. Brief II, *Toys Advertised Deceptively.* December 11, 1970. $5.00. Brief III, *Comments.* July 2, 1971. $5.00 Brief IV, *Reply Comments.* October 1, 1971. $5.00.

Federal Trade Commission Documents Filed by ACT. Testimony of Action for Children's Television Before the Federal Trade Commission. November 10, 1971. $5.00. *Petition to Prohibit Advertisements for Children's Vitamins on Children and Family Television Programs.* November 10, 1971. $5.00. *Petition to Prohibit Advertisements for Toys on Children's Television Programs.* December 15, 1971. $5.00. *Petition to Prohibit Advertisements for Edibles on Children's Television Programs.* March 22, 1972. $5.00. *Complaints on Specific Vitamin Pills.* May 1972. $5.00 *Supplementary Filing Relating to ACT Petition to Prohibit Advertising of Edibles on Children's Television.* January 1973; plus *Complaints on Specific Food Products.* March 1973. $5.00. *Comments on Proposed Guides Concerning Use of Endorsements and Testimonials in Advertisements,* March 1973, $5.00 (Charges to cover xerox and mailing.)

Foundation for Character Education (Boston). *Television for Children.* 1966. Pamphlet, 81 pages, 30¢.

JENNINGS, RALPH. *Programming and Advertising Practices in Television Directed to Children.* Prepared for Action for Children's Television, 1970. Xerox, 81 pages, $5.00.

JENNINGS, RALPH and CAROL. *Programming and Advertising Practices in Television Directed to Children—Another Look.* Prepared for Action for Children's Television, July 1, 1971. Xerox, 84 pages, $5.00.

MELODY, WILLIAM. *Children's Television: The Economics of Exploitation.* New Haven: Yale University Press, 1973.

MENDELSON, GILBERT and YOUNG, MORRISSA. Network Children's *Programming: A Content Analysis of Black and Minority Treatment on Children's Television.* Prepared for Action on Children's Television, August 1972. 21 pages, $5.00.

Second National Symposium on Children and Television. October 1971. Transcript of Speeches, $5.00.

Testimony Before U.S. Senate Commerce Committee. On "TV Violence." March 1972. $1.00.

Testimony Before U.S. Senate Select Committee on Nutrition and Human Needs. March 1973. $1.00.

"Who is Talking to Our Children?" Third National Symposium

on Children and Television at Yale University, October 1972. Transcript of speeches and workshops. 64 pages, $5.00.

YANKELOVITCH, DANIEL. *Mothers' Attitudes Toward Children's Television Programs and Commercials*. Prepared for Action for Children's Television. March 1970. Xerox, 37 pages, $5.00.

BOOKS, PAMPHLETS AND STUDIES ON CHILDREN'S TELEVISION NOT AVAILABLE FROM ACT

Action for Children's Television. Edited transcript of the First National Symposium on Children and Television, held October 16 and 17, 1970. New York: Avon Books, 1971.

AMBROSINO, LILLIAN and FLEISS, DAVID. *An International Comparison of Children's Television Programming*. National Citizens Committee for Broadcasting, July 1971. (NCCB, 1914 Sunderland Place, S.W., Washington, D.C. 20036.)

ATKINS, CHARLES K., MURRAY, JOHN P., and NAYMAN, OGUZ B. *Television and Social Behavior: An Annotated Bibliography of Research Focusing on Television's Impact on Children*. Bethesda, Md.; National Institute of Mental Health, Publication No. 2099, 1971.

BARNOUW, ERIC. *The Image Empire: A History of Broadcasting in the United States*. 3 vols. New York: Oxford University Press, 1970.

BOGART, LEO. "Warning: The Surgeon General has Determined that TV Violence is Moderately Dangerous to Your Child's Mental Health." *The Public Opinion Quarterly* 36 (Winter 1972–73).

BROWN, LES. *Television: The Business Behind the Box*. New York: Harcourt, Brace and Jovanovich, 1971.

Children and TV: Television's Impact on the Child. Association for Childhood Education International, 1967. (ACEI, 3615 Wisconsin Ave., N.W., Washington, D.C. 20016.)

Doing the Media. Center for Understanding Media, 1972. (CFUM, 267 W. 25th St., New York, N.Y. 10001.)

FEINSTEIN, PHYLLIS. *All About Sesame Street*. New York: Tower Publications, 1971.

FESHBACK, SEYMOUR, and SINGER, ROBERT D. *Television and Aggression*. San Francisco: Jossey-Bass, 1971.

FRANK, JOSSETTE. *Television: How to Use It Wisely with Children*. New York: The Child Study Association of America, Inc. 1969. Revised Edition. (CSAA 9 E. 89th St., New York, N.Y. 10028.)

GATTEGNO, CALEB. *Towards A Visual Culture*. New York: Outerbridge and Dienstrey, 1969.

GERZON, MARK. *A Childhood for Every Child: The Politics of Parenthood*. New York: Outerbridge and Lazard, 1973.

HALLORAN, JAMES, ed. *The Effects of Television*. New York: Panther Books, 1970. Chapter "Television and Education."

HALLORAN, JAMES, BROWN, R. L., and CHANEY, D. C. *Television and Delinquency*. New York: Leicester University Press, distributed by Humanities Press, 1970.

HERRMANN, ROBERT O. *The Consumer Behavior of Children and Teenagers: An Annotated Bibliography*. New American Marketing Association, 1969.

HIMMELWEIT, HILDE T., OPPENHEIM, A. N., and VINCE, PAMELA. *Television and the Child*. London: Oxford University Press, 1958. Reprint of chapters 1–4. (Available from Television Information Office, 745 5th Ave., New York, N.Y. 10022.)

JOHNSON, NICHOLAS. *How to Talk Back to Your Television Set*. Boston: Little, Brown and Co. 1970.

A. J. KAHN, B. KAMERMAN, B. G. MCGOWAN, eds. *Child Advocacy: Report of a National Baseline Study*. New York: Columbia University School of Social Work, 1973.

LESSER, GERARD S. *Children and Television: Lessons from "Sesame Street."* New York: Random House, 1974.

LIEBERT, ROBERT M., NEALE, JOHN M., and DAVIDSON, EMILY S. *The Early Window: Effects of TV on Children and Youth*. New York: Pergamon, 1973.

MACCOBY, ELEANOR E. "Effects of the Mass Media." *Review of Child Development Research*, September 1970.

Mass Media and Violence. Reprint of the National Commission on the Causes and Prevention of Violence, Vol. XI, 1969. (Available from Superintendent of Documents, U.S. Government Printing Office, Washington, D.C. 20402.)

MAYER, MARTIN. *About Television*. New York: Harper & Row, 1972.

MORRIS, NORMAN S. *Television's Child.* Boston: Little, Brown and Co., 1971.

MUKERJI, ROSE. *Television Guidelines for Early Childhood Education.* (National Instructional Television, Box A, Bloomington, Indiana 47401.)

New Directions in Children's Television. TV Quarterly, IX:3, (Summer 1970). 77 pages. (Available from National Academy of Television Arts and Sciences, 54 W. 40 St., New York, N.Y. 10018.)

PANNITT, MERRILL, ed. *TV and Your Child.* Series from 1969 issue of *TV Guide.*

PEARCE, ALAN. *The Economics of Children's Television Programming.* Washington, D.C.: Federal Communication Commission. 1972.

The Politics of Broadcasting. The Alfred I. duPont–Columbia University Survey of Broadcast Journalism, 1971–1972. New York: Thomas Y. Crowell Co., 1973.

PROWITT, MARSHA O'BANNON. *Guide to Citizen Action in Radio and TV.* New York, 1971. (Office of Communication, United Church of Christ, 289 Park Ave. South, New York, N.Y. 10010.)

SCHRAMM, WILBUR, LYLE, JACK, and PARKER, EDWIN B. *Television in the Lives of Our Children.* Stanford: Stanford University Press, 1961.

SHAYON, ROBERT LEWIS. *The Crowd Catchers: Introducing Television.* New York: Saturday Review Press. 1973.

Television and Education. Compiled bibliography. November 1962. (Television Information Office, 745 5th Ave., New York, N.Y. 10022.)

Television for the Family. National Association for Better Broadcasting, Vol. XII, No. 1 (Winter 1972). (NABR 373 North Western Ave., Los Angeles, Calif. 90004.)

Television and Social Behavior. A Technical Report of the Surgeon General's Advisory Committee on Television and Social Behavior. Washington, D. C.: U.S. Govt. Printing Office, 1972. Vol. 1: *Media Content and Control,* Papers and Reports, edited by G. A. COMSTOCK and E. A. RUBENSTEIN. Vol. 2: *Television and Social Learning,* Papers and Reports, edited by G. A. COMSTOCK and E. A. RUBENSTEIN. Vol 3: *Television and Adolescent Aggressiveness,* Papers and Reports, edited by E. A. RUBENSTEIN, G. A. COMSTOCK, and J. P. MURRAY.

Vol. 5: *Television's Effects: Further Explorations*, Papers and Reports, edited by G. A. COMSTOCK, E. A. RUBENSTEIN, and J. P. MURRAY.

WARD, SCOTT. *Effects of Television Advertising on Children and Adolescents*. Cambridge, July 1971. Marketing Science Institute, 1033 Mass. Ave., Cambridge, Mass. 02138.)

CABLE TV

Organizations

Cable Information Service, Rm. 860, 475 Riverside Drive, New York, N.Y. 10027. Publishes monthly newsletter.

Cable TV Information Center, 2100 M St. N. W., Washington, D.C. Publications available to community groups.

Founders Annex Public Service Project, P.O. Box 504, Beverly, Mass. Publishes information about cable ownership.

National Cable Television Association, 916 16th St. N.W., Washington, D.C. 20006. The major association for cable broadcasters.

Office of Communications, United Church of Christ, 289 Park Ave. S., New York, N.Y. 10010. Gives advice; publications.

Publications

BAER, WALTER S. *Cable TV: A Handbook for Decision-Making*. Rand Corp., 1700 Main St., Santa Monica, Ca. 90406, February 1973. Clearly written, textbook-style explanation of cable technology, with tables and diagrams. Covers cable economics, options for those contemplating ownership, local responsibilities, and public access.

Citizens Cable Council of Madison and Dane County: Community Action Handbook. P.O. Box 5574, Madison, Wisconsin 53705. A grassroots history of one community's experience in the development of a cable TV system locally.

FCC Regulations on Cable, FCC, Washington, D.C. 20554. Free.

The Here, Now and Tomorrow of Cable Television in Education: A Planning Guide. Prepared as a study of the Massachusetts Advisory Council on Education, 182 Tremont St., Boston,

Mass. Outstandingly useful source of information for those interested in ensuring that cable TV will be actively involved in education.

PRICE, MONROE, and WICKLEIN, JOHN. *Cable Television: A Guide for Citizen Action.* Pilgrim Press, 1505 Race St., Philadelphia, Pa. 19102. The ABC of involvement in community cable.

Sloan Commission on Cable Communications: *On the Cable: The Television of Abundance.* New York: McGraw-Hill Book Co., 1971. Scholarly analysis of cable TV's future possibilities.

TATE, CHARLES. *Cable Television in the Cities: Community Control, Public Access and Minority Ownership.* The Urban Institute, 2100 M St., N.W., Washington, D.C. 20037. Useful handbook.

CONSUMER EDUCATION

Recently many new consumer education materials have been reaching the teaching arena. The following are a selection of consumer education materials presently available.

"But First, This Message." 16mm. color film (15 min.), produced by Cinemagraphics for ACT. Deals with TV programs and ads, including quotes from children and professionals. Available for rental or purchase from ACT, 46 Austin St., Newtonville, Mass. 02160.

Consumer Action Now. 30 East 68th St., New York, N.Y. 10021. Monthly newsletter.

Consumer Education Bibliography. Prepared by the Office of Consumer Affairs and the New York Public Library, September 1971. Superintendent of Documents, U.S. Government Printing Office, Washington, D.C. 20402.

Consumer Education Materials Project. Consumers Union, E.S.D., Orangeburg, N.Y. 10962. Six books: *Early Childhood Consumer Education; Elementary Level Consumer Education; Secondary Level Consumer Education; Consumer Education in Jr. and Community Colleges, Postsecondary Vocational and Technical Institutes; Preparing the Consumer Educator; Adult Consumer Education in the Community.*

"Can You Borrow a Cookie?" 21-Inch Classroom, 55A Chapel Street, Newton, Mass. 02160. Five short consumer education television plays for K–4 accompanied by five-week curriculum package including teacher's manual.

Home Economics and Consumer Education. Benchmark Films Inc., 145 Scarborough Road, Briarcliff Manor, N.Y. 10510. "A Chemical Feast" (11 mins.); "Brand Names and Labelling Games" (9 mins.). Two short 16 mm. color films, with TV consumerist Marshall Ephron providing information with humor.

Instructor Magazine. Instructor Park, Dansville, N.Y. 15537. *Consumer Education in Your Classroom.* October 1972. Contains bibliography of materials for classroom use.

Media & Consumer. P.O. Box 1225, Radio City Station, New York, N.Y. 10019. Consumer journal, published monthly.

National Television Advertisers. 3245 Wisconsin Avenue, Berwyn, Ill. 60402. Lists major TV advertisers, with addresses.

TELEVISION AND EDUCATION

Organizations

Center for Understanding Media, 75 Horatio St., New York, N.Y. 10014. Headed by John Culkin, the Center provides a range of educational materials and services related to media education for both adults and children.

National Association of Media Educators, Room 308, 2000 P Street N.W., Washington, D.C. 20036. Provides a newsletter and information for professionals in the field of media education.

National Instructional Television, Box A, Bloomington, Ind. 47401. The central repository for all public television's educational programing; provides information.

Television Information Office (affiliated with the National Association of Broadcasters), 745 Fifth Ave., New York, N.Y. 10022. Provides information about programing, presented from point of view of the commercial broadcasters.

Publications, Materials for Teachers

ALLEN, DON. *The Electric Humanities.* Dayton, Ohio: Pflaum/ Standard, 1971. Collage of suggestions for teaching popular culture, literature, theater, music, and the total environment.

BROWN, ROLAND G. *A Bookless Curriculum.* Dayton, Ohio: Pflaum/Standard, 1972.

BERGER, ARTHUR ASA. *Popular Culture.* Dayton, Ohio: Pflaum/ Standard, 1972. Text and booklet demonstrating design of a secondary school course on popular culture, involving use of audiovisual techniques and creative efforts by students.

Children Are Centers for Understanding Media. Association for Childhood Education International, 3615 Wisconsin Ave. N.W., Washington, D.C. 20016. Pamphlet with articles by different authors describing elementary and secondary school media projects, and with list of resources for further study.

Doing the Media. The Center for Understanding Media, Inc., 267 West 25th Street, New York, N.Y. Portfolio of activities and resources for classroom use.

Exploring Television. Prepared by Loyola University Press, 3441 North Ashland Ave., Chicago, Ill. 60657. 1971. Secondary school worktext and teacher's manual.

FRANSECKY, ROGER B., and DEBES, JOHN L., eds. *Visual Literacy: A Way to Learn—A Way to Teach.* Association for Educational Communications and Technology, 1201 Sixteenth Street N.W., Washington, D.C. 20036. 32-page pamphlet and bibliography covering film, photography, and television.

HERMAN, DELDEE M., and RATCLIFFE, SHARON A., eds. *Radio, Television and Films in the Secondary School.* Skokie, Ill.: National Textbook Co. 1972. Curriculum Guide outline for course of study, divided into individual units which may be used as part of other courses.

HOGINS, JAMES BURL, and BRYANT, GERALD A., JR., eds. *Juxtaposition—Instructor's Manual.* Palo Alto, Calif.: Science Research Associates, Inc., College Division.

HOLMGREN, ROD, and NORTON, WILLIAM, eds. *The Mass Media Book.* Englewood Cliffs, N.J.: Prentice-Hall, 1972. Articles providing a critical overview of mass media.

LITTELL, JOSEPH F., ed. *Coping with the Mass Media.* Evanston, Ill. McDougal Littell & Co. 1972. Articles on television, movies, newspapers, taken from a high school language-study series.

————. *The Language of Man.* Evanston, Ill.: McDougal Littell & Co.

Learning: The Magazine for Creative Teaching. Learning, 530 University Ave., Palo Alto, Calif. 94301. Nine issues per year, monthly column on television.

LINTON, DAVID and DOLORES. *Practical Guide to Classroom Media.* Dayton, Ohio: Pflaum. 1971.

MANUEL, J. J., ed. *A Common Wealth: Views in Massachusetts Humanities.* Urbana, Ill.: National Council of Teachers of English. Articles describing the aesthetic and technological processes of humanities education, and four humanities programs, with a brief section on media.

Mass Media. Prepared by Loyola University Press, 3441 North Ashland Ave., Chicago, Ill. 60657. 1972. Secondary school worktext and teacher's manual.

Media and Methods. North American Publishing Co., 134 N. 13th Street, Philadelphia, Pa. 19107. Periodical published nine times per year.

PERKINS, W. H. *Teaching and Learning—A Critical Appraisal of the Mass Media with Particular Reference to Film and Television.* ERIC Reports ED 049 202, 1969. ERIC Processing and Reference Facility, 4833 Rugby Ave., Bethesda, Md. 20014.

Persuasion. Prepared and published by Loyola University Press, 3441 North Ashland Ave., Chicago, Ill. 60657. 1970. Secondary school worktext and teacher's manual.

PTST. Prime Time School Television, 100 North LaSalle St., Chicago, Ill. 60602. Background materials and bibliographies relating to documentaries and specials on prime-time television to help teachers make the best use of programs in the classroom.

Scholastic Teacher. Elementary Teachers' Edition or Junior/ Senior High Teachers' Edition, Subscription Dept., 902 Sylvan Ave., Englewood Cliffs, N.J. 07632. Periodical published nine times per year with "Tele-guide" section on TV specials.

Teachers' Guides to Television. Published by Broadcasting Association's Television Information Office. P.O. Box 564, Lenox Hill Station, New York, N.Y. 10021. Periodical published twice yearly giving background material on children's television programs of special interest to students.

VALDES, JOAN, and CROW, JEANNE. *The Media Works.* Dayton, Ohio; Pflaum/Standard, 1973. Worktext and companion logbook for secondary school use.

WHITE, DAVID MANNING, ed. *Pop Culture in America.* A New York Times Book. Chicago: Quadrangle Books. 1970.

WHITE, WILLIAM P., and GLESSING, ROBERT J. *Mass Media: The Invisible Environment.* Chicago: Science Research Associates, Inc.

AGREEMENT BETWEEN LANSING COMMITTEE FOR CHILDREN'S TELEVISION (LCCT) AND GROSS TELECASTING, INC.

The following agreement was sent as an official letter to Mr. Ben F. Waple, Secretary of the Federal Communications Commission on September 4, 1973. It was signed by the President of LCCT and the Chairman of Gross Telecasting.

Gross Telecasting, Inc., licensee of WJIM-TV in Lansing, Michigan, has been constructively engaged in a dialogue with two citizen's groups that have expressed a concern and interest in Lansing area broadcasting. Out of these sessions there has emerged an understanding which all parties agree should be reduced to writing and made part of the station's official FCC file. The two groups referred to are the Lansing Committee for Children's Television (LCCT) of East Lansing, Michigan, and Citizens United for Better Broadcasting (CUBB) of East Lansing, Michigan. LCCT is a member of CUBB. LCCT is joining with Gross Telecasting, Inc., as a signatory to these accords. As a result of discussion and review, LCCT and Gross Telecasting, Inc., are in agreement as follows:

1. Three representatives of LCCT appointed by that group will be included on the WJIM Public Service Advisory Board by January, 1974.

2. These three members and an additional two members of the LCCT Advisory Board (selected by LCCT) with three members of the existing board will be appointed to serve as a subcommittee on children's television.

3. Station management-level personnel will meet once every three months during the license period with this subcommittee on children's television. Both parties will be available for additional meetings based upon a written presentation of meaningful agenda items.

4. Consultation with this subcommittee shall include, but not be limited to:

A. Assisting WJIM-TV with the selection of syndicated programs for the late afternoon (4:00–6:00 P.M.) and early evening (7:00–8:00 P.M.) hours. It is understood that the final selection of such programs is the sole responsibility of the station. However, the large child audience available after school and in the early evening will not be ignored when the station plans its programs for this time period.

B. Consulting with WJIM-TV on any locally produced children's programing developed by the station during the coming license period.

C. Specifically advising and assisting in the development of a locally produced, daily (Mon.–Fri.) children's program. This daily program will be a minimum of 30 minutes in length and will begin on or before September 1, 1974. Consultation with LCCT on the research and development of this program will begin on or before October 1, 1973. It will be scheduled between 4:00 and 6:00 P.M. This program will go beyond children's need for mere escapist entertainment and sensitively deal with needs relative to a child's emotional, intellectual, social and physical growth and development WJIM-TV will hire a producer-writer for this program.

5. WJIM-TV will present a monthly children's special featuring children from the Lansing-Jackson-Flint area. LCCT will assist WJIM in seeking out desirable topics and assist WJIM in making contacts with the desired participants in the Lansing area only. These specials will begin on a monthly basis not later than January, 1974. These specials will be scheduled between 7:00 and 8:00 P.M. on a week night or between 6:30 and 8:00 P.M. on Sunday. So long as the time period falls within the above range it can be adjusted on a month-to-month basis.

6. Dr. Charles Atkin of the Michigan State University Communication

Department and a member of LCCT has agreed to undertake a study of the "cluster commercial" concept on a daily, locally produced children's program outlined in 4-C above. The station agrees to a trial of the "cluster" concept on this program for a minimum of 60 days commencing September 1, 1974. This period can be extended to 90 days if such extension is necessary to validate the study in the view of Dr. Atkin. Copies of Dr. Atkin's completed study will be submitted to both the LCCT Advisory Board and WJIM-TV representatives. These two parties will discuss the advisability of continuing the clustering of commercials after the 90-day trial period expires.

7. The station will develop local public service announcements featuring events, programs of interests, and needs of children in the WJIM service area. LCCT and LCCT's Advisory Board will bring to the station's attention subject matter and consult with WJIM-TV on these announcements whenever possible.

8. With regard to the daily children's program and the monthly children's specials: once commenced, these programs will be scheduled nine months of each year during the coming license period. They will not be scheduled in June, July, or August.

9. The purpose of this accord is to set aside prescribed time periods for locally produced children's programing as outlined herein. Adjustments of formats, talents, etc., will undoubtedly be necessary for maximum effectiveness. Effectiveness of the program will not be measured solely in terms of profit but must take into account the positive impact of the program on children. While the station will consult on a reasonable basis with LCCT, it is understood that the production of the programs must remain under the sole control of the licensee.

10. WJIM-TV will remove "Wild, Wild West" January 1, 1974, or earlier if possible. WJIM-TV will not reschedule "Wild, Wild West" in the 3:30–8:00 P.M. hours. WJIM-TV in replacing this program will consult with the subcommittee on Children's Television before selecting the replacement (as outlined in 4-A).

The parties signify that the above fairly represents their understanding by signing in the space provided below. On the basis of satisfactorily concluding this agreement with Gross Telecasting, Inc., the Lansing Committee for Children's Television recommends that renewal of the station's TV license is in the public interest.

National Association for Better Broadcasting (NABB) Comprehensive Guide to Family Viewing for 1974

COMMERCIAL NETWORK CHILDREN'S SHOWS

ABC AFTERSCHOOL SPECIALS — Monthly. Twelve programs spaced four weeks apart, and well worth waiting and watching for. Almost all of these have been outstanding. They could stand multiple reruns. For example, "Santiago's Ark" (repeated November 14 from an earlier showing), and any of several others from this series would make excellent family viewing programs in evening prime time.

ADDAMS FAMILY — NBC, Saturdays. One out of nine "new" shows "re-created" in animation for the Saturday children's hours. More than the others, except for "Star Trek," this retains the tone and flavor of the original cartoons and live-action series.

AMAZING CHAN AND THE CHAN CLAN — CBS, Sundays. Story content is based on crime, but this is not brutal or sadistic. It is just inept, shallow, and tiresome.

AMERICAN BANDSTAND — ABC, Saturdays. Dick Clark and guest stars with leading rock groups. Today's music and today's dance techniques, with enthusiastic participation by today's teens. For years the Clark show has kept pace with current styles in youth-oriented music.

BAILEY'S COMETS — CBS, Saturdays. Noise and action for action's sake on roller skates. A race around the world. Constant trickery. A waste of time.

BRADY KIDS — ABC, Saturdays. Using the same introduction as the evening show, this animated version has even less substance than its live-action progenitor. Characters are stereotypes. Production is mediocre.

BUGS BUNNY — ABC, Saturdays. Fast action. Production of these old segments is superior to today's limited animation in most series. Characters emerge unharmed from being slugged, clubbed, thrown, and blown up. Okay for family viewing, but poor and confusing fare for younger children unattended.

BUTCH CASSIDY — NBC, Saturdays. Animation is stiff and unreal in this show which involves a cartoon rock star in criminal and violent situations. Cassidy's singing talents used as a cover for investigative assignments. Cliché story situations. Unsuitable for children.

CAPTAIN KANGAROO — CBS, Monday–Friday mornings. Captain Kangaroo (Robert Keeshan) and his staff have performed a monumental service with this program over the past many years. Also the Columbia Broadcasting System deserves acclaim for keeping this on the air in the face of sometimes opposing economic pressures. This is commercial television's outstanding regular show for preschoolers. As such, it merits the network's continuing policy of supporting "Captain Kangaroo" against efforts to use its valuable time periods for more financially rewarding news or other adult programing.

CHILDREN'S FILM FESTIVAL — CBS, Saturdays. An anthology of films with special appeal for children. Quality is uniformly excellent. Most films are produced overseas. Introductions are done inimitably by Kukla, Fran, and Ollie. Will entertain adults as well as the kids.

EMERGENCY PLUS 4 — NBC, Saturdays. Animated from the live-action evening "Emergency!," this loses most of its values in the transition. In this, the fire department paramedics are aided in rescues by a group of youngsters. This effort to make the show referable to the Saturday A.M. audience also put the young characters in constant peril. Situations are at times unrealistic. Educational aspects of illustrating rescue techniques do not come across. Not recommended.

FAT ALBERT AND THE COSBY KIDS — CBS, Saturdays. Serious social problems, even traffic in dope, treated from point of view of black youngsters in urban setting. An appealing program that uses Bill Cosby's low-key guidance to good advantage. Unusual values in characterization and story content for animated series. Superior to shows making current season debut.

FLINTSTONE COMEDY SHOW — CBS, Saturdays. The Flintstone characters in brief segments complete in themselves. Sequences of rock music are integrated into the half-hour program. Production is routine, which means not very good.

FUNKY PHANTOM — ABC, Saturdays. Animated episodes based on stories from Revolutionary period. The derivations are silly and slapstick. Poor history—poorer show.

GO! — NBC, Saturdays. Live-action documentary-style series covering wide variety of topics such as a day in the life of a policeman, the flying aces of World War I, etc. A well-produced program of interest to older youngsters.

GOOBER AND THE GHOST CHASERS — ABC, Saturdays. Animated nonsense with Goober (a dog who can make himself invisible) and the Partridge family kids. Sinister characters and some frightening moments. Unsuitable for children.

IN THE NEWS — CBS, Saturdays. These are 90-second mini-news stories produced in documentary style by the CBS News Department. Several each Saturday morning. So superior in quality and content to the network's surrounding entertainment morass, it is hard to believe these are produced by the same network for the same audience.

INCH HIGH PRIVATE EYE — NBC, Saturdays. A gimmicky animated show with a Tom Thumb character operating in a full-sized world, except that the stories and situations are shrunken to minus size. The laugh track, incredibly using adult "laughers," is intrusive.

JEANNIE — CBS, Saturdays. This is based on the live-action "I Dream of Jeannie" series, with principals now juveniles to fit the Saturday morning audience. Whatever creative qualities there might have been in the original are missing from the Hanna-Barbera animated version. In making the characters younger the producers have gone too childish and silly even for the much younger viewers for whom this is intended. A complete disregard or contempt for the intelligence of the viewing children and adolescents.

THE JETSONS — NBC, Sundays. Animated series featuring space gadgetry. In story and treatment a distinct cut above the ordinary weekend show for children. Nevertheless, this show, like "The Flintstones," is strong on male/female stereotypes. The gimmicks are fun. The roles are not.

JOSIE AND THE PUSSYCATS IN OUTER SPACE — CBS, Saturdays. Animated chase, smash, weird intrigue. Characters are ugly. The production is crude. Unsuitable for children.

KID POWER — ABC, Sundays. Reruns of one of the most promising animated series of the preceding season. Superior to almost all current shows for youngsters. Characters are from Morrie Turner's "Wee Pals."

LASSIE'S RESCUE RANGERS — ABC, Saturdays. This is an outrageous animated destruction of whatever values the live-action "Lassie" series might contain. Not only that, the manufacturers of this rubbish have incorporated violence, crime, and stupidity into what is probably the worst show for children of the season.

LIDSVILLE — NBC, Saturdays. Live-action costume fantasy, with characters who live in hats. Not much story. The program may appeal to very young children.

MAKE A WISH — ABC, Sundays. A show of unusual merit produced by the public affairs departments of ABC News with writer Lester Cooper and producer Tom Bywaters. The program is enchanting, stimulating, and visually refreshing. "Make A Wish" illustrates what children's TV can be when it is produced by competent people with a real interest in their audience.

MISSION: MAGIC! — NBC, Saturdays. Eerie settings and music. Robbery, gangs, and other sordid ingredients in cheap and mediocre animation. Unsuitable for children.

MULTIPLICATION ROCK — ABC, Saturdays. These short segments, along with "Grammar Rock," etc., are interspersed through the ABC Saturday morning periods. They are delightful—far superior to anything else on the A.M. schedule. Animation, music, and content show what commercial TV *can* do for children in the rare instances when networks and producers combine to do something really first-class.

MY FAVORITE MARTIANS — CBS, Saturdays. They threw out the baby and saved the dirty bath water. Everything bright and clever from the live-action "My Favorite Martian" is gone from this shoddy animated transition. Inane, silly, and witless to the point of vulgarity.

NATURE'S WINDOW — Syndicated. Although these beautiful five-minute wildlife vignettes are usually integrated into children's programs with varying content and formats, the NABB committee is impelled to point out again that these are delightful, and well worth seeking out. More than 100 species of North American birds and animals are filmed in natural color. There are 130 segments. Recommended without reservation.

THE OSMONDS — ABC, Sundays. Reruns, but these are better than most of the current cartoon series. The Osmond singing group. Routine art work, but the characters are not ugly, which is a switch from typical T.V treatment.

SCOOBY DOO MOVIES — CBS, Saturdays. An hour-long show using "guest stars" in animation each week. Everything from Don Knotts to Batman. A lot of action and many situations that scare younger children. Tired material rehashed from countless other kid shows.

SIGMUND AND THE SEA MONSTERS — NBC, Saturdays. Fantasy live action featuring two "human" boys and a sea monster who becomes their pal. Plot is inconsequential.

SPEED BUGGY — CBS, Saturdays. Animated, apparently patterned after the deceased live-action series "My Mother, the Car." Anyway, "Speed Buggy" has human characteristics up to a point. "Stories" deal with trickery and amiable criminals engaged in various forms of deceit and destruction.

STAR TREK — NBC, Saturdays. Compared with other new animated shows the opening episodes have been impressive. More care has gone into this in production, story treatment, and characterization.

THE STARLOST — NBC, Saturdays. This is a syndicated series produced in Canada, and it may vary in time and station placement in various cities. As a rare entry from our northern neighbor it would be welcomed on the U.S. schedule, except that its beginning is inauspicious. It has been talky and overcomplicated. There have been episodes that are just plain dull, others that have too high a degree of frightening incidents to be acceptable for the children to whom the program is directed.

SUPER FRIENDS — ABC, Saturdays. Superman, Batman, Aquaman, Wonder Woman, and other superheroes with their violence, crime, and fantastic powers have been generally dropped from network schedules since the public and professional furore against such shows that climaxed in 1969. Now ABC has crept back with a package that on the surface seems to be relatively innocuous. Begin with the title: It's now "Super FRIENDS!" Some of the evil in the adversaries of the superheroes is gone. Likewise some of the crime and the excesses in destruction. But these people are still the superrace: the all-powerful, the apparently benign totalitarians whose mission is to "fight injustice, right that which is wrong, and serve all mankind." When the President of our nation has trouble he can't handle, he passes the job along to Superman, Batman, Aquaman, and Wonder Woman. When our established institutions and constituted authorities are helpless, we call on the Super Friends in their Great Hall of Justice. We delegate to them all our responsibilities to protect ourselves and our neighbors against a world full of weird menaces. They always save us. We don't need anybody else. Everything is settled by the violent use of super power. That's the message.

SUPERSTAR MOVIE — ABC, Saturdays. These are animated hour-long treatments based on pre-established shows and showmen such as Yogi Bear, Jonathan Winters (he's everywhere), the Bewitched people, and others. Opener for the current season was a reprise of "Lost in Space." Unfortunately, few if any creative elements have been added, and the show is essentially a warmed-over rehash of second-rate material.

VISION ON — Syndicated. This is a half-hour British Broadcasting Corporation series that won the grand prize as best children's TV show at Munich's 1972 International Children's Television Festival. In the U.S. in October, 72 stations were carrying the series, which is distributed by Time-Life Films. It is a highly creative program designed for hard-of-hearing youngsters. It will entertain kids and adults, deaf or not. It combines animation, live-action pantomime, and other techniques, with emphasis, of course, on the visual. Highly recommended.

PUBLIC STATIONS AIR
SUPERIOR CHILDREN'S FARE

With exceptions as noted in the alphabetical listings of network and syndicated shows, the superior programs for children are generally aired in the United States by the noncommercial public broadcasting outlets. There are four current noteworthy programs circulated chiefly through PBS outlets. These are:

MISTER ROGERS' NEIGHBORHOOD, the gentle and appealing program that was originated by Fred Rogers in April 1954 on public station WQED, Pittsburgh. An enduring program that utilizes fine creative talents in writing, performance, and production.

SESAME STREET, continuing to grow as it begins its fourth season with 12 million U.S. children between the ages of three and six. The 130 hour-long segments of the new season are being aired by 200 public and 50 commercial stations. "Sesame Street" this year has a $5.6

million budget for research, production, and distribution. It is produced by Children's Television Workshop.

ZOOM!, the fascinating live-action, half-hour series produced by Christopher Sarson at WGBH-TV in Boston. One of the most creative and entertaining shows for children ever produced.

THE ELECTRIC COMPANY, another Children's Television Workshop program, in its second season. This year there will be 130 half-hour segments in this extensive experiment to help meet the problem of reading failure among elementary school children. CTW has a $7 million budget for this project.

All of the above programs are highly recommended by the NABB committee for the children and teens to whom they are directed.

COMMERCIAL NETWORK PRIME-TIME SHOWS AND SELECTED SYNDICATED PROGRAMS

ABC SUSPENSE MOVIE — Saturdays. These are made-for-TV melodramas that are high on crime and action but usually low in plot structure and depth of characterization. Poor fare for youngsters.

ADAM 12 — NBC, Wednesdays. Police officers shown as competent professionals and human beings. Constructive values for young viewers in forming attitudes toward law enforcement.

ALL IN THE FAMILY — CBS, Saturdays. Bright entertainment for those who enjoy an uninhibited assault of bigotry and other human foibles. Early episodes of the new season have seemed to give a harsher and more noisy conflict among the characters than in preceding years. The NABB committee suggests that parents assess the impact of the program on their individual children. Families with young children may want to evaluate Archie's expressions against their own language standards.

AMERICA — Syndicated. Don't miss it, even though you may have seen all or part of it on NBC last year. It is now syndicated throughout the U.S., and is usually spotted in better time periods for family viewing. Excellent for everyone. A tribute to American history and traditions that is much needed today.

APPLE'S WAY — CBS, Sundays. This new show is being produced by the same people who are responsible for "The Waltons." It is concerned with an architect who returns with his wife and four children to live in his home town in Iowa. Unfortunately, it competes head-on with NBC's "Wonderful World of Disney." But that's the network way.

BARNABY JONES — CBS, Sundays. A gimmicky crime thriller, with Buddy Ebsen miscast as a private eye, with scripts that are devoid of demands on anybody's creative talents.

BONANZA — Syndicated. This years-long series, canceled last year by NBC, is now in syndicated release. It is possibly the best of all TV westerns, but parents should know that many episodes are too violent for unattended young children.

BRADY BUNCH — ABC, Fridays. Trivia in a background in which there are no economic problems and in which all situations are superficial. Escapism for youngsters. Pleasant enough, but no real substance. Something to think about: this has one of the largest audiences of children and teens of any show on the air.

CAROL BURNETT SHOW — CBS, Saturdays. This show is now mercifully scheduled at a late hour. It is funny and the entertainers are top-flight, but the show is too uneven in taste to be suitable as family entertainment. It's just right for the corner bar.

CANNON — CBS, Wednesdays. Cannon is an interesting character. For mature viewers this is an interesting melodrama. Okay in its present time period, but look out for the day when it will be off network and syndicated, probably five times per week, in time periods readily accessible to children.

THE CHASE — NBC, Wednesdays. Just what the title says. Crime and brutality with all the production gimmicks to lend excitement for viewers who want action regardless of story depth or continuity. Routine cops-'n'-robbers. Again the network places this in an early evening time period and thumbs its nose at the social scientists who have proven a causal relationship between the viewing of excessive violence and antisocial behavior.

CHOPPER ONE — ABC, Thursdays. Cops in helicopters.

COLUMBO — NBC, Sundays (alternate weeks). A good melodrama. Crime and some violence, but the emphasis is on Peter Falk's characterization and his deductive investigations.

COUSTEAU SPECIALS — ABC. Magnificent photography. These rank with TV's finest programs. Don't miss them.

THE COWBOYS — ABC, Wednesdays. This is to replace the non-lamented "Bob & Carol & Ted & Alice."

THE DATING GAME — Syndicated ("access time"). Cheap and distasteful. Poor attitudes and sleazy examples for youngsters.

DIRECTIONS — ABC, Sundays. This has been around a long time, and it deserves to stay on indefinitely. Provocative treatment of social problems, including such topics as "the dignity of death."

DIRTY SALLY — CBS, Fridays. It's a spin-off from "Gunsmoke" featuring a frontier female trash collector and a reformed gunfighter.

DOC ELLIOT — ABC, Saturdays. This looked like a winner when we saw the pilot in March 1972. It has been changed slightly in treatment and locale, but it has James Franciscus, warm and intelligent scripts, and beautiful exterior backgrounds. Hopefully this will be treated kindly by the network, allowed to grow, and maintained in a time period convenient for family viewing.

DUSTY'S TRAIL — Syndicated. Trivia, but so was Gilligan's Island, which also had Bob Denver. Conceivable that this could last. If there's anything to it, harmful or otherwise, we haven't discovered it.

EMERGENCY — NBC, Saturdays. This may appeal to the ambulance chasers among us, but it is well produced and it has its positive values in illustrating how paramedics can rescue victims of emergency situations. Questionable for unattended children. Constructive show for family viewing.

THE F.B.I. — ABC, Sundays. Once again the NAAB committee points out that this association has continuously opposed the presentation of commercial entertainment under the official endorsement of local, state, or national governmental bureaus. "The F.B.I." is not only an illustration of the misuse of official support, it is also excessively violent and sordid in story content. As often as not the F.B.I. is unwittingly portrayed as inept, with solutions achieved by sheer luck and last-second rescues of terrorized victims of criminal action.

FIREHOUSE — ABC, Thursdays. Content is indicated by the title.

GIRL WITH SOMETHING EXTRA — NBC, Fridays. Sally Field in a transition from flying nun to a girl who has no embarassment whatever at reading the inner thoughts of her husband on their wedding night. She's come a long way. But he can't stand her "invasion of his privacy." A gimmick show, probably not long for this world.

GREAT DAY! — CBS, Fridays. To replace the cancelled "Roll Out!" Maude's maid (Esther Rolle) and her grouchy husband (John Amos) in a spin-off series from "Maude," which itself was begat by "All in the Family."

GUNSMOKE — CBS, Mondays. Of course there wasn't much law in those days, but even so the marshal probably was not always out of town when real trouble was brewing. And it's not likely that all the women who operated girl-equipped saloons were as delectable and true-blue as Kitty. "Gunsmoke" has rolled along all these years on myths and appealing characterizations, but its beginning to show, not its age, but its fundamental lack of depth. It may be nearing its network demise. If and when that happens, it will likely go on forever and ever in syndicated release to stations everywhere, unless parents become alert to the true content of such programs. But how can that happen, when the parents of tomorrow are the ones who watched these shows yesterday?

HALLMARK HALL OF FAME — NBC, intermittent schedule. This is Hallmark's 23rd consecutive season of sponsorship *and production* of this most esteemed of all television programs.

HAPPY DAYS — ABC, Tuesdays. This is a situation comedy about a family of five, replacing the suspended "Temperatures Rising."

HAWAII FIVE-O — CBS, Tuesdays. A very bad show for youngsters of all ages, strategically scheduled to lure a very large youth audience. Graphic horror. Such things as a close-up on a girl as she dies horribly from bubonic plague. A man brutally shot spits on his attacker to give him the plague . . . and then there are rats, etc.

HAWKINS — CBS, Tuesdays (monthly). A 90-minute show that gives some range for Jimmy Stewart's talents. Well-produced from intelligent scripts. Top-flight casts. Adult content, aimed at older, i.e. Jimmy Stewart fans. The best of the new season's melodramas.

HEC RAMSEY — CBS, Sundays (alternates with McMillan and Wife, McCloud, and Columbo). Richard Boone as a rugged western lawman who introduces new techniques in crime detection. Interesting for adults. Too violent for younger children.

HERE'S LUCY — CBS, Mondays. Lucy is television's past, present, and future. If the tapes don't disappear she'll be here forever.

HOLLYWOOD SQUARES — Syndicated. A bright and funny show, usually aired in prime-time "access" periods. Entertains, in spite of lavish prizes and excessive commercialism. This is the best example of a game show that is a planned performance, not a contest.

IRONSIDE — NBC, Thursdays. Detective melodrama a cut above most other crime shows. Good entertainment for adults. Okay for older youngsters, if viewing with family.

BRIAN KEITH SHOW — NBC, Fridays. Somehow, this show doesn't quite come off, even with the title change from last season's "Little People." Keith appears uncomfortable in his role. The producers haven't determined whether this is for children or adults. If they'll do a show that is for *both*, or for *either*, they might have a winner. At present this uses trite predictable situations and rides along on stereotype characterizations.

KOJAK — CBS, Wednesdays. An expertly produced and performed crime melodrama. Okay for adults who enjoy this type of show, but much too sordid in content and violent in action for children and impressionable juveniles.

KUNG FU — ABC, Thursdays. This is a difficult show to recommend from a viewpoint of acceptability for youngsters. It preaches nonviolence but it contains a lot of brutality and sadism, and it stirs strong feelings in the viewers for retaliatory vengeance. Carradine is excellent as the fugitive Chinese priest. The stories are tense and exciting. In the opinion of the NABB committee, this is far too strong and disturbing for unattended children.

LASSIE — Syndicated. There are hundreds of Lassie episodes included in different series packages. Some are fine: some have much less value. NABB recommends that parents take a look before deciding suitability for their children.

LET'S MAKE A DEAL — Syndicated ("access time"). A frantic, low-grade show that has no legitimate place in prime-time television. Plays on the unpleasant characteristics of participants and viewers.

LOTSA LUCK — NBC, Fridays. Incredible bad taste, unless such gag lines as "I feel Olive should do the christening" of a newly installed toilet are now in vogue in the nation's living rooms at seven and eight in the evening. Maybe NBC should launch a bathroom network. The other two networks have taken over the bedroom. This is too tasteless for most living rooms. The characters are not the sort of people you would invite over for your youngsters to meet.

LOVE, AMERICAN STYLE — ABC, Daytime. Finally canceled from its late evening weekly period, this continues as a daily afterschool trap for youngsters who should not be exposed to this shoddy and superficial way of learning about sex relations in general. "Love, American Style" illustrates questionable patterns and life styles. The episodes are often funny, but they are full of ex-burlesque gags.

THE MAGICIAN — NBC, Tuesdays. Routine melodrama. Expensive production. Spectacular chase sequences, with graphic violence to the limit of what network censors will allow. Unsuitable for youngsters.

MANNIX — CBS, Sundays. Rough-and-tough crime drama. Uses psycho criminals in sordid story situations. A part of the CBS all-violent shows for Sunday evening. (There will be some relief when the short-lived Perry Mason show is replaced in February.)

MARCUS WELBY, M.D. — ABC, Tuesdays. This has always been a quality show. It is expertly produced drama with authentic professional backgrounds. This is okay in its late time period. It is not good for children to learn about illness from TV.

DEAN MARTIN SHOW — NBC, Thursdays. Self-indulgent attitudes toward sex and excessive drinking. The music is pleasant and entertaining. The show is like a stag party that leads up to, but never quite reaches, the climactic moments for which these parties are produced. Adults only.

M*A*S*H* — CBS, Saturdays. There has been criticism from some that "M*A*S*H" glorifies war. The NABB committee believes, however, that the program is a sharp and very funny satire on the stupidity and futility of armed conflict. We believe also that the series has improved in this new season, and that it is one of the highlights of the week's schedule. It is intended for adults, and parents must make a decision regarding the acceptability of this show for their children.

MAUDE — CBS, Tuesdays. This show has been the center of controversy, largely due to the two episodes that were concerned with Maude's abortion. The program is complex and it is difficult to evaluate in terms of its suitability for children and teenagers. It disturbs some families both for its viewpoints on social issues and its deliberately open approach to situations that have traditionally been matters for whispered inner-sanctum consideration. The NABB committee considers "Maude" to be entertaining and provocative, and believes that decisions about control of viewing should be made in individual homes.

McCLOUD — NBC, Sundays (alternates with McMillan and Wife, Columbo, and Hec Ramsey). Dennis Weaver in the title role of a light melodrama that emphasizes McCloud's character and eccentricities. Unsuitable for unattended children.

McMILLAN AND WIFE — CBS, Sundays (alternates with McCloud, Hec Ramsey, and Columbo). Reminiscent of the "Thin Man" movies, though not so tightly written. Light, satiric treatment. Not suitable for children.

MEDICAL CENTER — CBS, Mondays. They used Julie Harris in the premiere episode, but they did not eliminate the agonizing soap-opera treatment that has been a continuing characteristic of this undistinguished series. A poor way for youngsters to learn about the practice of medicine.

MARY TYLER MOORE SHOW — CBS, Saturdays. Bright, intelligent, and beautifully produced. An outstanding cast. Real people—adults, for a change—you'd be happy to have your child visit.

BOB NEWHART SHOW — CBS, Saturdays. This show made its debut just last season. It is now entrenched as a sophisticated comedy that gives full expression to Newhart's unique talents. First-rate production. Fine cast.

ODD COUPLE — ABC, Fridays. A funny show for adult audiences. At 8:30 P.M. Fridays (7:30 P.M. Central Time), however, there are millions of youngsters at the TV sets across the land . . . and this follows the kid-happy "Brady Bunch," and is followed by "Room 222."

OWEN MARSHALL: COUNSELOR AT LAW — ABC, Wednesdays. This series continues as one of the week's most provocative dramas. It features thoughtful treatment of very strong story themes. Characters are developed with an understanding of human frailties. Recommended for adults and mature teens.

THE PARTRIDGE FAMILY — ABC, Saturdays. This relatively light-weight show is unfairly pitted against CBS' "All in the Family," but it is pleasing entertainment for youngsters. Music has a special appeal for preteens.

POLICE STORY — NBC, Tuesdays. No doubt the best of the season's oversupply of crime dramas. Believable characters involved in believable police action situations. Not for children, but this can be good entertainment for adult audiences. Martin Balsam stars.

POLICE SURGEON — Syndicated. This is aired during prime-time "access" periods, and it is a major reason for such programing being in disrepute. Scripts and production are mediocre. Morbid, sordid. and brutally violent. Junk.

THE PRICE IS RIGHT — Syndicated. A game show that has as its lure lavish prizes. Superior, however, to such debacles as "Let's Make a Deal." Price information is interesting.

THE PROTECTORS — Syndicated. Third-rate, excessively violent series that is still around in prime-time "access" periods in some cities. Entirely unsuitable for children.

THE ROOKIES — ABC, Mondays. Close-up coverage of brutal killings and other forms of refined violence, such as the choking of a nun by a psycho who is really a nice guy trying to win a place on the kidney dialysis machine for a dying girl by eliminating those who are already getting treatments on the limited equipment. Stories and characters are a front for the graphic violence that gives this show its morbid appeal. The kids should never see it.

ROOM 222 — Syndicated (or ABC daytime). This is an excellent series just leaving the network's evening schedule. Watch for reruns in other hours.

SANFORD AND SON — NBC, Fridays. This is near the top in the ratings, and it has the outstanding talents of Redd Foxx and Demond Wilson. A funny and worthwhile show, but the NABB committee would like to see characters not quite so close to stereotypes and situations further removed from slapstick.

SHAFT — CBS, Tuesdays. Ninety-minute films alternating with "Hawkins" on Tuesday evenings. This features black star Richard Roundtree. The formula is rough melodrama, with many incidents of graphic violence. A laundered version of the movie on which the series is based, with any real story values washed out.

SNOOP SISTERS — NBC, alternate Tuesdays. A stylized, unabashed other-era handling of deductive crime investigation, played vigorously by Helen Hayes and Mildred Natwick. The show is funny and entertaining. The producer is Leonard Stern, talented veteran of tongue-in-cheek story treatment.

THE SIX-MILLION DOLLAR MAN — ABC, Fridays. This is being moved into the early Friday evening spot as a regular feature for America's youngsters. It's a perfect illustration of the Superman concept, plus all the gore and brutality that go with a program manufactured to emphasize all facets of gratuitous violence. The hero, who claims to be "more than the sum of his parts," is a monstrosity constructed from recycled parts of other humans after he himself was ripped to pieces in an explosive crash. This show is rebuilt from pure rubbish, and it is in no way superior to any part of its accumulated junk.

SONNY AND CHER — CBS, Wednesdays. A year ago the NABB committee felt that parts of this program were in questionable taste for juvenile viewers. This season the show seems to be more tasteful. Production, performance, and talent are first-class.

STREETS OF SAN FRANCISCO — ABC, Thursdays. Graphic violence and psycho characters treated with the Quinn Martin touch for this type of horror. Bad for youngsters of any age.

TEMPERATURES RISING — ABC (unscheduled). This was an awful show a year ago, and ABC scheduled it for the new season. It improved so much that the network quickly canceled it. But it is to return at an unannounced date. With Paul Lynde, it is a funny program.

THRILL SEEKERS — Syndicated ("access time"). Dangerous spectacular stunts by glamorized "heroes" who risk their necks for pay or, as the title suggests, for the thrills involved. Might induce youngsters to emulate reckless useless risks. As far as the NABB committee has observed, no consequences of destructive "accidents" among the thrill seekers are shown.

TOMA — ABC, Thursdays. Action melodrama with a tough but appealing cop in the leading role. Psycho characters, who are really nice guys bent on serving society, are the villains. Routine crime, except that it might touch off slaughter for kicks, as the ABC Sunday night film "Fuzz" apparently ignited the Boston horror and other incidents a few weeks back.

TREASURE HUNT — Syndicated ("access time"). If you can stand eight regular commercial spot announcements, plus another 22 products plugged for prizes for the contestants, then watch the dispensation of prizes through chance without requirements of skill or intelligence, then maybe this is for you. Others would be better off with the set switched off.

DICK VAN DYKE SHOW — CBS, Mondays. Again this season, neither very bad nor very good. Let's hope that before old age overtakes them completely Van Dyke, Hope Lange, and Carl Reiner find a show worthy of their potential talents. Their program this year is based on sex situations, but whose isn't.

WAIT TILL YOUR FATHER GETS HOME — Syndicated ("access time"). Whatever else can be said about this show, it is unquestionably the most intriguing weekly half-hour animated series on television, including anything they do for the children on Saturday mornings. The characters are clear-cut; the dialogue sharp and satiric. It's for adults, but mature youngsters will enjoy it, too.

THE WALTONS — CBS, Thursdays. Last year at this time, when "The Waltons" was off to an uncertain and faltering start, we wrote here that the show would run for years if the network gave it a real chance to build a following. Now success is assured. Excellent writing, production, and performance. Characters are warm and referable. Millions of youngsters watch each week with their families. The program is even better this season.

LAWRENCE WELK SHOW — Syndicated. Welk and his music. Production is good. He has many fans.

ORSON WELLES GREAT MYSTERIES — Syndicated ("access time"). This series deals with crime and horror, but it is devoid of graphic violence and the treatment is so stylized that most episodes appear to be acceptable, even for children if they are viewing with other family members.

WILD KINGDOM — NBC, Sundays. This is a family show. It is listed here rather than under "children's programming" because it has strong appeal for adults as well. Photography is first-rate. Producers have a real concern for wild and endangered species.

WILD WORLD OF ANIMALS — Syndicated. This Time-Life series is probably the most beautiful and authentic nature program on the air. Narration, with solid information and without contrived sensationalism, is done by William Conrad. Episodes viewed have been fascinating. Highly recommended.

FLIP WILSON SHOW — NBC, Thursdays. Probably the smoothest and most appealing variety show on TV. Flip Wilson is personable and very funny. Production is excellent. Acceptability for family viewing is a matter of taste. In shows watched this season by the NABB committee questionable material has been kept to a minimum.

THE WORLD AT WAR — Syndicated. Hour-long episodes comprising a documentary of World War II. This is difficult to evaluate, because its impact will largely depend on the attitudes and reactions of individual viewers. For the perceptive, the war is set forth with all of its horrors. For those to whom warfare is a game and violence a source of emotional thrills, the effects might be an entirely different matter. Therefore, this is recommended by the NABB committee with reservations. The documentation is massive, and drawn from opposing sources in history's greatest war.

YOUNG PEOPLE'S CONCERTS — CBS, (intermittent schedule). The best, always. Several very special shows each year. Of equal appeal to youngsters and adults.

WONDERFUL WORLD OF DISNEY — NBC, Sundays. This is a series that consistently maintains standards in production and in story material. When literary classics are aired, however, the Disney scripts have often altered basic content. Scenic backgrounds and wildlife photography are outstanding.

WORLD OF SURVIVAL — Syndicated. This is a wildlife series featuring studies of species threatened with extinction through man's neglect. John Forsythe is narrator. Produced with aid of World Wildlife Fund. Recommended.

EXCESSIVELY VIOLENT SHOWS IN SYNDICATION

All the programs listed here are old series with a comman pattern of human degradation as a lure to attract thrill-seeking immature viewers. Most of them were produced by or for networks. They are now distributed in the syndication market throughout the world. They are grouped here as a quick guide to many of the oldest highly objectionable programs. Many other crime programs call for individual evaluations. They follow, listed alphabetically.*

Old Excessively Violent Crime Westerns

BAT MASTERSON
BRANDED
THE CALIFORNIANS
CHEYENNE
CIMARRON STRIP
COLT 45
COWBOY G-MEN
CUSTER
THE DAKOTAS
FRONTIER DOCTOR
GUNS OF WILL SONNETT
HAVE GUN, WILL TRAVEL
IRON HORSE
JESSE JAMES

KIT CARSON
LARAMIE
LAWBREAKER
LAWMAN
LONE RANGER (films)
THE LONER
MAN CALLED
SHENANDOAH
RANGE RIDER
RAWHIDE
THE REBEL
RIFLEMAN
RIVERBOAT
SHOTGUN SLADE

* The program descriptions are reprinted from the Winter 1972 and Winter 1973 issues of the *Better Radio and Television* quarterly of NABB.

STAGECOACH WEST	TOMBSTONE TERRITORY
STORIES OF THE CENTURY	TRACKDOWN
TALES OF TEXAS RANGERS	TWENTY-SIX MEN
TALES OF WELLS FARGO	WANTED, DEAD OR ALIVE
THE TEXAN	ZANE GREY THEATER

Old Excessively Violent Crime Programs

THE AVENGERS	MR. AND MRS. NORTH
THE BARON	MR. LUCKY
BOURBON STREET BEAT	OFFICIAL DETECTIVE
BURKE'S LAW	PETER GUNN
CODE THREE	RICHARD DIAMOND
THE DEPUTY	THE SAINT
THE DETECTIVES	SECRET AGENT
FELONY SQUAD	SHERIFF OF COCHISE
GREEN HORNET	STATE TROOPER
HAWAIIAN EYE	SUNSET STRIP
HIGHWAY PATROL	SURFSIDE STRIP
HONEY WEST	TIGHTROPE
M-SQUAD	YANCY DERRINGER
MIKE HAMMER	

Listed below are 140 program series produced for television. Many of these series are comprised of upwards of 100 hour and half-hour episodes. Even so, the programs listed here constitute only a part of the arsenal of crime and violence which remains as the chief stock-in-trade of broadcasters throughout the land. There are many hundreds of crime and horror movies that are aired over and over again in non-network daytime and evening time periods. There are excessively violent series still in circulation that are not listed here. Then there are the current network made-for-TV melodrama movies and the current regular crime series which fill close to half of the network's prime-time hours.

THE ADVENTURER — Bizarre and excessively violent. Unbelievable situations. Unsuitable for children.

ADVENTURES IN PARADISE — This series is not excessively brutal, but it is too rough for younger viewers. Crime in the South Pacific. Ninety hour-long episodes.

AMAZING THREE CARTOONS — Animated. Creatures from outer space. Children involved in terrifying situations. Poor production.

ASTRO BOY CARTOONS — A worthless, nightmarish cartoon series. Boy robot fights crime.

ATOM ANT — A super insect with violent solutions for all problems. Unsuitable for child audiences.

GENE AUTRY SHOW — Excessive violence in a crime-and-killing-are-fun format. Old, but it's still around.

THE AVENGERS — Stylized, explicit sadism. Often scheduled in early evening hours. This is far too bizarre for younger viewers.

BATMAN (Live-action) — When this series was produced for ABC, the network claimed that it was basically satiric humor, but the children do not respond to *Batman* as funny. The lure is violence and morbid suspense. The show disparages social values.

BATMAN CARTOONS — Rubbish.

THE BIG VALLEY — ABC first scheduled this in late evening hours when its extreme violence and frequently sordid themes, were not easily accessible to children. Now it gets multiple showings each week in early hours.

BIRDMAN — Mad scientists and elaborate gadgetry. Violent action with superman theme. Originally aired by NBC.

COMBAT — War with a touch of reality. Much violent action, with tense and frightening situations, along with compassion for individuals involved. Unsuitable as entertainment for younger children alone.

COOL McCOOL CARTOONS — Tedious animated repetition of slapstick violence. At best a waste of time.

DANIEL BOONE — This former NBC Thursday evening mainstay is above average for TV westerns, with scenery and characters intriguing for children. Unfortunately, it is unsuitable for unsupervised children because of excessive violence, historical inaccuracy, and the depiction of youngsters in danger.

DASTARDLY AND MUTTLEY — Ugly, noisy, and full of pointless violence, this is a contrived formula show derived from past animated mediocrity.

DEATH VALLEY DAYS — An unusual western with positive qualities in story and characterizations. Occasional excessive violence makes this unsuitable for unattended children.

DEPARTMENT S — A British melodrama involving a mysterious Interpol agency. Druggings, sluggings, murders . . . with a Paris background. Production quality is better than for some crime series, but this is essentially just another part of the violence avalanche.

DR. DOOLITTLE CARTOONS — Animated blight from the NBC network. Kid-show formula with no creative qualities and no relationship to the original Dr. Doolittle story. Random educational items are meaningless in this shoddy surrounding.

EIGHTH MAN CARTOONS — Grotesque. Frightening. Robots, disguised as men, have superior powers. A prime example of irresponsible programing by any broadcaster who chooses to put it on the air.

EIGHTY-EIGHTH PRECINCT — Police melodrama. Better than average, but too sordid and violent for children.

FANTASTIC FOUR — Highly objectionable for children with weird super "things" and frightening situations. This animated mediocrity was first aired by ABC.

FANTASTIC VOYAGE — Violent pseudo-science with constant menace. Formula junk produced for network TV's Saturday morning children's ghetto.

FELIX THE CAT — Old and violent. Mad scientists.

FIREBALL XL5 — Clever production techniques wasted in a show that is tense, excessively violent, and full of evil characters.

FLASH GORDON — If there is a worse show anywhere, the NABB committee has yet to discover it. Terror, torture, cliffhanger suspense.

THE FUGITIVE — Entertaining melodrama for mature audiences. Not for children.

GARRISON'S GORILLAS — Extreme violence unacceptable for child audiences. Language and action are rough and brutal.

GIGANTOR CARTOONS — Grotesque, ugly, and discredited. Gigantor is a robot controlled by a boy who helps the inept authorities. Much violence.

GIRL FROM UNCLE — Explicit horror. Torture for fun. Produced by and for NBC, now syndicated.

GROOVY GOOLIES — Grotesque and ugly, this is a noisy, forced animated series featuring monsters. Ridicule and torture for fun. Explosions. Destruction.

GULLIVER — Tiny bad guys against tiny good guys. All the charm of the Gulliver classic is lost in this transition to formula TV animation. Unsuitable for children.

HARBOR COMMAND — An old series. Crime around the harbor. Better than most such shows.

HECKLE AND JECKLE — Rowdy, chase-type animated violence.

HELP, IT'S THE HAIR BEAR BUNCH — An ugly Hanna-Barbera cartoon series with humanoid animals escaping from the zoo and outwitting authorities.

HERCULOIDS — Originated for CBS, this is a distasteful, mediocre, menacing animated show dominated by fantastic creatures.

HIGH CHAPARRAL — Extreme violence and brutality in many episodes. Not at all suitable for children.

ALFRED HITCHCOCK SHOW — Horror with the Hitchcock trademark. Macabre satire that is sordid and terrifying for juveniles.

HOGAN'S HEROES — An irresponsible mockery of documented historical tragedy. The Nazis were not comic buffoons, nor were World War II prisoners a joke. This is an unwholesome show that illustrates war as a setting for fun and harmless adventure.

I SPY — Well-produced melodrama with Bill Cosby and Robert Culp. Now unfortunately aired several times per week in late afternoon or early evening hours. Violence and adult story lines make this a poor choice for unsupervised children.

THE INVADERS — Tense melodrama. Hostile creatures from a doomed planet invade earth. Not for children.

IT TAKES A THIEF — Crime with a tongue-in-cheek approach that appeals to adults but is not for children. Now syndicated, it is often scheduled in early hours.

JONNY QUEST — Outstanding animation to depict crime, terror, and violence. A waste.

JOURNEY TO THE CENTER OF THE EARTH — This show, first aired by ABC, is one of the most repulsive animated series ever made. Terrifying situations with children in constant peril.

KIMBA CARTOONS — Art quality is good, but content is not suitable for children. Small animals in stories that illustrate the superman theme.

KING KONG — An old animated series with disobedient child who commands huge ape. Negative values.

LANCELOT LINK/SECRET CHIMP — This show, with live chimps as characters mouthing childish "lines," and with very old cartoons integrated into a variety format, is contrived and ugly. Unacceptable as entertainment for children.

LANCER — Hour-long crime westerns. Unsuitable for children.

LAND OF THE GIANTS — Technically unimpressive and obviously subjected to budget limitations. Little people and giants. Crime and violence are dominating factors. This is a gimmick show highly objectionable for child audiences.

LAREDO — Far too violent for youngsters, but tongue-in-cheek treatment and amusing characters will appeal to many adults.

LONE RANGER (LIVE ACTION) — Crime and violence in large measure. Unsuitable for children.

LONE RANGER CARTOONS — A crude distillation of the bad elements of the Lone Ranger live-action show. Animated and excessively violent mediocrity.

LONGSTREET — Well-produced detective melodrama with interesting locations. Star's blindness, instead of adding values and depth to story treatment, is used as a gimmick to increase the suspense.

LOST IN SPACE — Poor-quality science fiction. Bad family pattern for young viewers in that children are disobedient, care is not taken by adults, and stories are left hanging. Nothing to recommend.

MAGILLA GORILLA CARTOONS — Noisy, heavy-handed cartoons produced by the Hanna-Barbera animation factory. Mediocre and insensitive. Objectionable for children.

MAN FROM UNCLE—Horror, sadism, and brutality. There is a veneer of ersatz comedy which gives this an altogether cynical approach so far as youthful viewers are concerned.

MARINE BOY CARTOONS — One of the very worst animated shows. Child characters in extreme peril. Expresses a relish for torture and destruction of evil characters.

MARK OF ZORRO — Old violent series. Better than most, but too tense and rough for younger children.

MARSHAL DILLON — Reruns of old "Gunsmoke" episodes. More violent than present network shows. (See "Gunsmoke.")

MAVERICK — One of the cleverest of TV westerns. Not for children, however. The hero is a professional gambler. Card cheating and other forms of trickery are presented as skilled accomplishments.

MIGHTY MOUSE CARTOONS — Poor-quality animation on the discredited superman theme. Cruelty. Continuous physical conflict.

MILTON THE MONSTER CARTOONS — Tasteless and grotesque animated monsters. Objectionable for children.

MISSION: IMPOSSIBLE — Murder and other forms of violence for fun. Characters are brutal and evil. Motivation is greed, rather than social reform. Original ingenuity of series has disappeared. Irresponsibly scheduled in early time periods in many cities.

MOBY DICK CARTOONS — Huge, horrible monsters. An ugly show with meaningless story content.

MOD SQUAD — They're always running and they are consistently at the center of the grimmest criminal action. Opponents are brutal and savage. The program lost the veneer of involvement in social issues which marked the series in its first seasons. Police action and policies would shame any self-respecting law-enforcement department. Certainly a bad show for children and younger teens.

MOTOR MOUSE/AUTOCAT — A little smart mouse and a big dumb cat in a stereotype hit-and-chase program from the Hanna-Barbera cartoon factory. Almost plotless. Noisy and violent.

THE MUNSTERS — Too grotesque for children. Grandpa is a vampire. Disturbing story themes.

NAME OF THE GAME — Story material is often unsuitable for youngsters. Plots involve social problems—teen drug use, establishment versus youth, campus revolt—but in melodramatic and sometimes shallow treatment. Production is lavish. At times clever, satirical.

N. Y. P. D. — A good police show. Strong drama and adult themes. Not suitable for youngsters.

O'HARA, U.S. TREASURY — Expertly produced melodrama based on fictitious activities of Treasury agents. Sordid themes. Racial angles are handled fairly and well. Foreigners are portrayed as people, not necessarily evil.

OUTER LIMITS — A pioneer program for nightmarish terror devices designed to lure juvenile audiences through fright and horror. Originated by ABC.

PENELOPE PITSTOP — Chase, violence, grotesque characters. Unsuitable for children.

PERRY MASON — Well-produced melodrama. Violence and story themes unsuitable for children.

THE PERSUADERS — Tony Curtis in a deplorable, distasteful exercise in stylized violence and crime. No concern for human life or human values. A very bad show for children.

PETER POTOMAS CARTOONS — Grotesque. Mediocre.

POPEYE CARTOONS — Rough and rowdy. Physical force settles all problems. Unpleasant values.

RAMAR OF THE JUNGLE — An atrocious live-action jungle series. Highly objectionable for children.

RAT PATROL — War-is-a-game violence. Historically distorted. Frightening.

RELUCTANT DRAGON AND MR. TOAD — Noisy, destructive, almost plotless cartoons. Worthless.

RIFLEMAN — There is appeal in the father-son relationship, but there's too much crime and violence for children.

ROBIN HOOD — Confusion of reality, fantasy, social values. Unsuitable for children.

ROCKET ROBIN HOOD — Animated space pseudo-science fiction. Extremely objectionable superman rubbish.

ROY ROGERS — A prime example of violence-for-fun entertainment. Murder, dull-witted reactions to story situations, and unacceptable philosophy.

RUN FOR YOUR LIFE — Better than average melodrama, but unsuitable for youngsters.

SAMSON AND GOLIATH — A dismal show with a super boy and a super dog. Crime.

SEARCH — In spite of all the tired gimmicks of hokum melodrama this is almost plotless. It is centered on a World Security Organization that is itself a dead-end trap for viewers searching for entertainment.

SHAZZAN CARTOONS — Child characters in constant peril. A bad show for youngsters.

SNUFFY SMITH (and other comic strip types) — These animated segments are widely distributed and aired within programs comprised of several varied elements. Animation seems to emphasize the less appealing aspects of familiar comic strip characters. Cartoons portray stereotypes of incompetent generals, illiterate mountaineers, etc. Shoddy entertainment for children.

SPACE GHOST CARTOONS — Outer space with children chased by evil monsters. Grotesque and frightening.

SPACE KIDETTES CARTOONS — Children menaced and terrorized by evil outer-space monsters.

SPEED RACER — An imported limited-animation crime series that is virulently violent. Unsuitable for children.

SPIDER MAN CARTOONS — Irresponsible terror program originated by ABC.

SUPER HEROES CARTOONS — Animated rubbish.

SUPER PRESIDENT — An all-time low in bad taste, with the President of the United States in a superman role. NBC was responsible for this direct ideological pitch for totalitarianism. We fear that there may be other broadcasters who are irresponsible enough to keep it in circulation.

SUPER SIX CARTOONS — Another NBC cast-off. Noisy, badly plotted, grotesque.

SUPERMAN CARTOONS — Disgraceful and irresponsible fare for the world's youngsters. Threadbare plots, unsuitable values. Children deserve better. First aired by CBS.

SUPERMAN FILMS — Murderous, excessively violent preachment of totalitarian ideology. Superman, as the benevolent dictator to his friends and the all-powerful destroyer of his enemies, has set the pattern for much of what is wrong with entertainment on commercial TV. Society, without Superman, is defenseless against the forces of corruption. The show distorts basic democratic concepts.

TARZAN — Thin and confusing story themes with a hokey jungle background. A poor show for small children.

THREE STOOGES (Live-action and cartoon) — Distasteful slapstick. crude and witless. Bad for children.

THUNDERBIRDS — Realistic puppet characters and supermodern gadgetry make this a fascinating show from a production standpoint. Stories are highly involved and very suspenseful. Centers on disaster and constant peril. Too tense for younger children.

TWELVE O'CLOCK HIGH — Wartime drama that does not stir man-to-man hatreds. Well produced. Adult themes. Recommended for mature audiences.

ULTRAMAN CARTOONS — Ultrabad animation of ultrabad story material.

UNCLE WALDO CARTOONS — Distasteful stereotypes in crime and violence, usually aired with other animated series. Not up to usual Jay Ward standards (i.e., "Bullwinkle").

UNDERDOG — Rough and violent action. Unsuitable for children.

THE UNTOUCHABLES — Vicious and brutal. When this was originated by ABC years ago, critic John Crosby called it the worst show ever made for TV. There is no reason to change this rating.

THE VIRGINIAN — A slow-paced western with attractive outdoor backgrounds. Some episodes are much too violent and tense for child viewers.

VOYAGE TO THE BOTTOM OF THE SEA — Originally produced by ABC when networks competed to originate the most nightmarish shows. A bad show for children, with fright-inducing devices built around incredibly far-fetched stories.

WAGON TRAIN (sometimes aired under "Trailmaster" title) — Good entertainment for adults who like this form of melodrama. Often too frightening for younger children.

WILD, WILD WEST — In Los Angeles and elsewhere this highly objectionable show is now running five or six times per week in early evening hours by irresponsible broadcasters. "Wild, Wild West" contains some of the most sadistic and frightening sequences ever produced for television.

ABOUT THE AUTHOR

Evelyn Kaye, a former newspaper reporter and feature writer and the mother of two children, was a co-founder and past President of Action for Children's Television, and is now its Publications Director.

Action for Children's Television (ACT) is a national organization dedicated to child-oriented quality television without commercialism. ACT was founded in 1968 in Newton, Massachusetts, and today has thousands of members across the country and the support of major institutions concerned with children.

The American Academy of Pediatrics is the pan-American association of physicians certified in the care of infants, children, and adolescents organized for the primary purpose of ensuring that all children of the Americas attain their full potential for physical, emotional, and social health.

Act Aims

· · · to encourage the development and enforcement of appropriate guidelines relating to children and the media;

· · · to pressure and persuade broadcasters and advertisers to provide programing of the highest possible quality designed for children of different ages;

· · · to encourage research, experimentation, and evaluation in the field of children's television.

For more information about Action for Children's Television, fill out the form below and send this page to ACT, 46 Austin St., Newtonville, Massachusetts 02160.

We are also interested in your views about children's television. If you wish, complete the questionnaire on the back of this page so that we can find out what really concerns you.

I would like more information about Action for Children's Television.

Name_____

Address_____

My special interest in this area is_____
_____
_____
_____
_____

1. I am the   mother   of   children
                father   (how many)

   Ages: _____
   (Answer questions in a different colored ink for each child
   between the ages of 2 and 11.)
2. The following answers refer to my child aged
3. How many hours of TV does your child watch each weekday
   (Monday through Friday) on the average
   How about Saturday?
   How about Sunday?
4. a) Do you think there are enough programs in your area
      designed specifically for children?
           Yes ☐   No ☐
   b) How often do you watch TV programs with your child?
      Never ☐   Quite often ☐   Occasionally ☐
      Almost always ☐
5. Which programs does your child watch most often? (List
   on separate sheet.)
6. In general, how would you rate these programs?
   Excellent ☐   Good ☐   Fair ☐   Poor ☐
7. There are commercials on children's TV programs at present.
   Would you prefer children's TV to have:
   a) No commercials?   ☐
   b) Fewer commercials?   ☐
   c) Commercials only at the beginning
      and end of program?   ☐
   d) No change in the present system?   ☐
8. How often has your child asked you to buy a TV-advertised
   cereal?
   a) Never (If you check this, skip to next question)   ☐
   b) Occasionally   ☐
   c) Frequently   ☐
   d) If he has, did you buy the cereal?
           Yes ☐   No ☐
   e) If you bought, were you satisfied?
   f) If no, why not? (Answer on separate sheet.)
9. What other concerns do you have about children and TV?
   (Answer on separate sheet.)